The Destiny of the Michael Community

The Archangel Michael

The Destiny of the Michael Community

Foundation Stone for the Future

Peter Selg

2014
SteinerBooks

STEINERBOOKS
AN IMPRINT OF ANTHROPOSOPHIC PRESS, INC.
610 Main St., Great Barrington, MA 01230
www.steinerbooks.org

Copyright © 2014 by Peter Selg. All rights reserved.
No part of this publication may be reproduced, stored in
a retrieval system, or transmitted, in any form or by any
means, electronic, mechanical, photocopying,
recording, or otherwise, without the prior
written permission of the publisher.

Originally published in German as *Grundstein zur Zukunft.
Vom Schicksal der Michael-Gemeinschaft.*
Published by Verlag des Ita Wegman Instituts 2013.
Translated by Marguerite Miller and Douglas Miller.

LIBRARY OF CONGRESS CONTROL NUMBER: 2014933143

ISBN: 978-1-62148-068-6 (paperback)
ISBN: 978-1-62148-069-3 (ebook)

Contents

Preface   7

1. "The evils hold sway..."
   The Laying of the Foundation Stone
   on September 20, 1913
   Lecture, Dornach, February 15, 2013   9

2. The Supersensible Michael Community
   and the Destiny of the Anthroposophical Society
   Lecture, Dornach, February 21, 2013   39

Notes   83

If understood correctly, the difficulties and problems [of the Anthroposophical Society] can strengthen the feeling that today the Anthroposophical Society—like nothing else in the world—requires our support and protection more than ever. Since the beginning of the twenty-first century, the battle for the future of the Anthroposophical Society founded at the Christmas Conference 1923/24—the spiritual teacher's greatest deed—has entered its decisive phase. Today the counterforces are rising up in an attempt to destroy this Anthroposophical Society by any means, even from within, and doing so with great force because they know this deed of Rudolf Steiner's cannot be conquered as long as it maintains and protects its connection with its spiritual roots.

—SERGEI O. PROKOFIEFF [1]

My brothers and sisters, fill your souls with a longing for a true spirit knowledge, for true human love, for strength of will.

—RUDOLF STEINER
Address at the laying of the foundation stone Dornach, September 20, 1913 [2]

Preface

This volume represents a response to a request for my summary of two lectures I held at the Goetheanum (Dornach, Switzerland) in February 2013. The first lecture (on the laying of the foundation stone of the First Goetheanum) was held during the annual meeting of the Swiss Anthroposophical Society; the second (on the supersensible Michael community) was held during an international conference concerned with the New Mysteries. Even though these two themes belong together or share an inner relationship, the context of a lecture requires a simplified treatment of the complex issues they raise. Nevertheless, I hope that this chance to evoke a memory of this subject can be helpful for the ongoing work of the anthroposophical movement. Once again, I owe a debt of gratitude to Sergei O. Prokofieff for his contribution to the substance of these lectures. Without him and his work these lectures would not have been held.

Peter Selg
Ita Wegman Institut
Arlesheim, Switzerland
Easter 2013

I

"*The evils hold sway...*"

The Laying of the Foundation Stone on September 20, 1913

Lecture in Dornach, February 15, 2013

I have no wish to evoke a sense of arrogance in anyone, but I would like to repeat a statement once made during a great event when mention was made of what was to happen through those souls that had taken up a task they were to carry out. These souls were told—not to arouse their pride, but in an appeal to their humility:
"*You are the salt of the earth.*"³

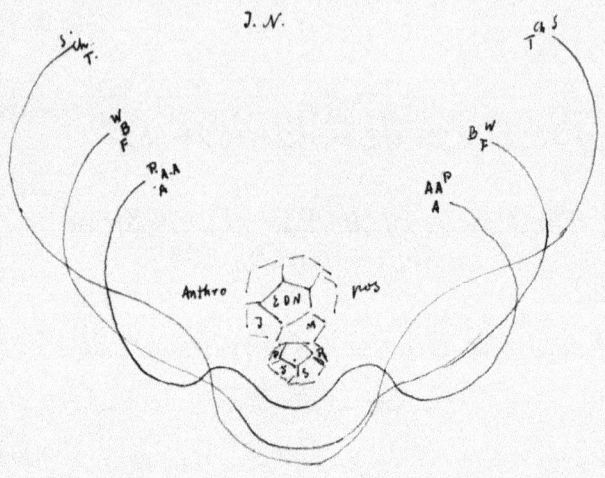

Rudolf Steiner: Draft of the Foundation Stone Document

"The evils hold sway..."

Dear friends,

In the years that followed the laying of the foundation stone of the first Goetheanum on September 20, 1913, Rudolf Steiner repeatedly recalled that event. The "ideas," the "feelings," and the "emotions" that lived in those souls present at the laying of the foundation stone during this "shared hour of celebration" were to be remembered; according to Rudolf Steiner, those "warmly glowing feelings" should be raised to consciousness.

He had already asked those in attendance on September 20, 1913, not only to be awake to the events surrounding the foundation stone laying, but also to take them up in the depths of their being, in the destiny dimension of their own existence: "Seek to inscribe in your souls the greatness of the moment we are going through this evening."[4] Thus Rudolf Steiner spoke about an inscription to be made and something that was to be "gone through"—that is, not simple presence of mind but an act of suffering, a process with a hidden unsettling or even painful quality. The consciousness of what was to be "gone through" should be maintained or continually renewed—that is, should never pass over into forgetfulness. Spirit recollection should be exercised concretely and joined to the will aspect of one's own existence—as future-oriented activity related to the world.

Rudolf Steiner hoped that the processes of consciousness he outlined would be pursued with intentional focus in the souls of individual anthroposophists (at the time of the foundation stone laying and in the sphere of their active memory); but also carried out in the realm of community, in a collaborative consciousness. These were not merely tasks for those individuals present at the laying of the foundation stone, but also for the community of the Anthroposophical Society—tasks at the core of what unites it, its very essence.

The laying of the foundation stone for the Dornach building was serious in every respect—in regard to what had been planned and what had begun as well as to the situation of the age in which it occurred. In his brief address during the evening hours of September 20, 1913, after the foundation stone had been laid, Rudolf Steiner said, "Guided by karma we stand at this moment in a place through which significant spiritual streams have passed: this evening, may we feel within ourselves the seriousness of the situation."[5]

The circle of people gathered around him was comparatively small and the event less than impressive—in and around a small trench with rain falling on a muddy hill near Basel. Nevertheless, what was taking place before the eyes and ears of the people gathered there was not merely an internal matter for the Anthroposophical Society nor for those in attendance. Instead, Rudolf Steiner asked those gathered there to direct their consciousness to the world situation in the present time, and especially to the human being within it. He spoke of the pressing need to spiritualize civilization, a need felt in our time as a yearning within countless human souls—even if only in the form of a generally vague and inadequate "hope for the spirit." "Look around you, my dear sisters and brothers, and see how this vague yearning, this vague hope for the spirit holds sway in humanity today!"[6] Rudolf Steiner explained how the spiritual longing of humanity is not obvious for the most part, how in itself it is not clear to people. They are not awake to where they are going nor to how they can determine their inner path; they are diverted from what is essential, and just below the surface they are filled with anxiety. Ahriman is blocking the view ahead, the way, the truth, and the life, and creating an unconscious fear of what is spiritual; this anxiety is part of the fundamental makeup of a modern, critical-skeptical humanity that stands at a distance from the world.

From various perspectives, the image of the future presented by Rudolf Steiner on the evening of September 20, 1913 (and in the commemorative addresses that followed), was more than bleak—"we are already confronted by times in which souls will be desolated because the spiritual atmosphere influenced by materialism gives these souls no life forces."[7] According to Rudolf Steiner, the soul-spiritual "desolation" will have its effect if we fail to succeed in creating an opening through which a powerful spiritual impulse can enter civilization:

> Young children today will encounter—not theoretically but in practice itself—an existence that relentlessly poses the question: What is the purpose of life? Why this desolate existence? The pallid countenances of those who are young children today—countenances distorted by need and suffering in life—will stand before our souls in the future; for these souls nothing is capable of gleaming through material life to offer them solace in the face of the desolation that can take hold in human life if materialism persists.[8]

According to Rudolf Steiner, questions about the meaning of life, about one's own existence and individual biography—questions active below the surface in every human soul—are deflected, muted, suppressed by the materialism that determines the course of our civilization. This was a situation the eyewitnesses to the laying of the foundation stone were not to ponder but *feel* and *suffer*:

> There ensues, my dear friends, that great sympathy, that encompassing compassion that surges in the soul, that

empathy with those who will come after—and who will be able to find the Earth livable only if what Spiritual Science offers has been prepared in the spiritual atmosphere of this our Earth.

Let us feel, my dear sisters and brothers, this anxiety.[9]

Rudolf Steiner spoke—without pathos—about a "cry," a "longing cry for the spirit" that we could not avoid hearing if the present situation is really understood. And this cry demands a real answer: "Let us feel ourselves surrounded by the souls of human beings in whom sounds the yearning cry for the spirit."[10]

~

With his presentations from the *Fifth Gospel* barely two weeks after the laying of the Dornach foundation stone, Rudolf Steiner would begin speaking about the childhood and youth of Jesus of Nazareth before the baptism in the Jordan—an ongoing and increasingly intense experience of suffering in view of the spiritual situation of humanity.[11] As depicted by Rudolf Steiner in Oslo and in later lectures in Germany, Jesus experienced the decay of the old Mystery religions and humanity's lack of a spiritual perspective, its decline into materialism, and its largely hopeless situation. Outwardly He met very little that was destructive or even catastrophic in the sensory-physical world. Nonetheless, Jesus of Nazareth recognized and felt that humanity and its life on Earth would encounter abysses if no new spiritual element entered in. He perceived the cries within the seeming silence[12]—a situation and experience that Rudolf Steiner himself passed through in the decades before the turn of the nineteenth century into the twentieth, although it was framed by different consciousness and historical conditions.[13]

"The evils hold sway…"

An utterly new beginning, a "macrocosmic illumination," had become necessary at the "turning point in time" in order for human evolution to continue in a good way and for the life forces on the Earth to be rescued.[14] Something similar could be found in the immediate present at the turn of the nineteenth to the twentieth century and during the pre-Michaelmas season in 1913, less than eleven months before the outbreak of a murderous, highly mechanized war that would last many years. It was a war that plunged the world into the abyss to an extent never before imagined, part of the "karma of materialism." ("In certain ways this war is the karma of materialism."[15]) Three months after the foundation stone was laid (and three months before his death on March 31, 1914), Christian Morgenstern wrote to his old friend Marie Goettling, a pastor's daughter from Soraus who viewed Anthroposophy with very little understanding:

> Just look at the world today, just compare it to the world of your youth. Add another fifty or eighty years, and the desolation will have spread so broadly that people would no longer desire to live if islands of spiritual life did not at least exist, if a diminishing minority did not *prepare the way* for that time. That is the help *we* have to provide, the help and the tragic need for it that you seem unwilling to grasp. It is the Christianity that calls us today, one that neither the official church nor the many forms of private Christianity—and these differ only slightly from the opinion of the church—are willing to recognize. Don't you see that something that is dying must be replaced by something new, that there are *new Christian deeds* because the old ones are no longer sufficient; that a *nova vita* must begin for one who acknowledges Christ. That *nova vita* will not only mean being good, doing good; it will *also*

look for approaches that support development. Only the right cultivation of these approaches can prevent goodwill, the best will, the greatest love, from ending in despair.

It is only possible to speak out of one's own experience; but when I do so, I must say I do not know where I would be today if my life had not been made understandable and bearable through the knowledge offered by theosophy. In despair, in madness, in a revolution, somewhere in a life of philistinism—perhaps not anywhere at all this side of the grave.[16]

A few years later Rudolf Steiner would designate the Dornach building as an "emblem" for the "breakthrough" of a new spiritual impulse in the development of the Earth and culture—an absolute necessity in order to get beyond the "dead point" that the progress of civilization had reached. "Anthroposophy is a path of knowledge that would lead the spiritual in the human being to the spiritual in the cosmos."[17]

∽

During July 1912—as Rudolf Steiner was producing his third Mystery drama (*The Guardian of the Threshold*) in Munich and writing his book *A Way of Self-Knowledge*—the First International Eugenics Conference was convened at University College in London. It was attended by almost 700 leading scholars (including physicians, biologists, anthropologists, philosophers, and theologians) and a number of politicians. Under the honorary chairmanship of Charles Darwin's son, the chairman of the British Eugenics Society, the conference focused on the genetic improvement of the human race and heredity through individual and governmental intervention—with birth control for "less valuable people" (prohibiting marriage and instituting sterilization) and an increased birth rate for those with "value." A positive selection principle was to be institutionalized at the governmental level, and the future "fitness of our race" was to be effectively insured.

Alfred Ploetz had already promoted this view in 1895, when he had supported the primacy of "race hygiene" and the "wellbeing of the race" above the wellbeing of the individual. In his 1895 publication *Die Tüchtigkeit unserer Rasse und der Schutz der Schwachen. Ein Versuch über Rassenhygiene und ihr Verhältnis zu den humanen Idealen, besonders zum Socialismus* (The capability of our race and the protection of the weak: An essay on race hygiene and its relationship to human ideals, especially to socialism), Ploetz, one of the leading German "eugenicists" and a significant personality at the London congress, included among other things a plea for a "gentle" death by morphine for weak or malformed children, and he recommended killing all twins and every child whose parents were older than forty-five (mother) or fifty (father), or who already had six children. All this was an example, or symptom, of the "spirit" of the time and an increasingly drastic—and dramatic—darkening of the human image and human consciousness.

Rudolf Steiner's work was diametrically opposed to this negation of human individuality; he warned about the horrendous dangers associated with the thought of "improved breeding" of the race or of the "national hereditary pool." "And the time will come, perhaps not long from now, when these tendencies will be developed further at a conference like the one that took place in 1912, when additional tendencies will appear."[18] "Materialism will quickly take its obvious next step…"[19]

With the establishment of the School for Spiritual Science, which would be housed in the building being constructed in Dornach (Switzerland), Rudolf Steiner hastily countered the dynamic of materialistic development. He saw the approaching destruction of Central Europe—not only as a political entity but also as a spiritual-geographic landscape in which thinking about human beings and their spirituality, value, and dignity had long been a central element of historical development. For centuries, German idealism—as well as many associated elements in literature, philosophy, religion, and aesthetics—had assured that the consciousness of the individuality and the rightful freedom of human beings would not be lost in a world progressively shaped by science; rather, it had been gradually cultivated in Central Europe.[20] During the nineteenth century, the forces at work in an accelerated materialism and positivism had nevertheless led to a point where this development had nearly come to a standstill and almost ceased; now, with social Darwinism, market economics, and racist thinking, these forces were approaching a decisive breakthrough.

At the laying of the foundation stone for the Dornach building, Rudolf Steiner spoke about the contemporary possibility that human will would no longer be able to help the Earth achieve the goal it had been given at the "primal beginning." This means that it could no longer be a place for the evolution of humanity and human development, but would instead end in self-destruction—in wars of all against all, or in technological-ecological catastrophes of epic proportions.

The building Rudolf Steiner was constructing in Dornach was intended to counter this materialistic tendency; it was not exclusively or even primarily a center for art and culture but for a new, practical thinking—about the human being and creation. From the beginning—starting with the intentions for a building in Munich—Rudolf Steiner had made unmistakably clear that the building to be constructed as a center for the anthroposophical movement was not to represent merely a conference center or theater in the narrower sense—for the staging of the Mystery dramas, for example. Instead, it would be nothing less than a school for Spiritual Science, or the home for such a school. Two years before the laying of the Dornach foundation stone, Rudolf Steiner noted in the first news sheet of the Johannes Building Association: "The thought of a School for Spiritual Science is the necessary outcome of the dissemination of spiritual knowledge—knowledge our time has been deemed worthy to receive."[21]

In principle, by October, 1911 the members of the German Section of the Theosophical Society should have been able to understand what this means. A new Michael Age had begun during the last third of the nineteenth century, a new epoch in humanity's development—humanity that was in a position to open wide the door for a new science of the spirit despite the continuing intensification of materialism and advance of technology in modern life. Since the beginning of the twentieth century, the audiences at Rudolf Steiner's theosophical-anthroposophical lectures and his readers had been able to witness step-by-step the unfolding of this Spiritual Science, a Spiritual Science of the "consciousness soul age." This Spiritual Science would establish in Dornach a center of schooling for spiritual research, education, and teaching; a school of advanced studies that would also be in a position to offer a new impetus to civilization and its various fields of endeavor.

Rudolf Steiner noted: "Today we have the task, I would say, of taking up—taking in—the full stream of spiritual life that comes to us from the heights."²² Then he spoke of the great task of the Anthroposophical Society and movement, a task that "consists of grasping the rays of a new spiritual light now available to humanity and impressing them on the way culture and civilization are conducted."²³

At the end of 1923, a little more than a decade after the first foundation stone laying in Dornach, the sole requirement Rudolf Steiner set for membership in the Society was recognition of the *need* for a "School for Spiritual Science." Any person could become a member "who sees something justifiable in the continuing existence of an institution such as exists in the School for Spiritual Science in Dornach."²⁴ *"The School of true Spiritual Science must exist here [in Dornach]."*²⁵ This School was to be centered and built upon the human being—on the fundamental knowledge of his true being within an age that increasingly overshadows this existence, distorts it, and shoves it into the background. "What is enkindled in us by anthroposophical Spiritual Science with its knowledge that strives toward the supersensible is human love that teaches us about human worth, love that allows us to feel human dignity."²⁶

At the laying of the foundation stone on September 20, 1913, Rudolf Steiner noted that this is a matter of fearlessly acquiring a belief and trust in "what the science of the spirit can proclaim"²⁷—to be able to work and act positively for the world based on this Spiritual Science ("...the wisdom and meaning of the new knowledge, the new love, and the new strong force must come alive in human souls").²⁸

~

The steps leading from the teachings of Anthroposophy—the body of knowledge found in the lectures and written works—to the construction of the building in Dornach were taken via the arts, and it was a path of action. In December 1911, Rudolf Steiner noted at the first general meeting of the Johannes Building Association in Berlin: "To begin, an answer to the question of whether Anthroposophy will be understood today very much depends in a certain broader sense on an answer we cannot provide in words, we cannot express with ideas—instead it depends on our turning to the deed."[29]

Rudolf Steiner first visited the parcel of land in Dornach during autumn 1912, following his Basel lectures on the Gospel of Mark. It was then that he walked the land and determined that it would be appropriate for the building. Soon after, he pressed for a radical change in direction; additional applications for permission to build in Munich were canceled, and a decision was made for Dornach. All else would follow from this.

In the summer of 1913, Rudolf Steiner produced the fourth of his Mystery Dramas, *The Souls' Awakening* (in which the ahrimanic tragedy makes an emphatic impact on the community around Benedictus). He also wrote *The Mysteries of the Threshold*, worked on the wooden model of the building, announced his lectures on the Fifth Gospel to be held in Oslo, and, in the first week of September, commissioned the metalworker and anthroposophist Max Benzinger to make the foundation stone from two copper dodecahedrons.

On September 17, three days prior to the act of laying the foundation stone, Rudolf Steiner surveyed the Dornach hill with a walking stick; he sought and determined the exact location for the foundation stone—including the Earth and the cosmos in an exact determination of what was needed: *"This is the spot."*[30] Then he asked that a trench 1.75 meters deep and six meters across be dug without delay; a protective cement container for the foundation stone needed to be prepared as well. Max Benzinger arrived in Dornach on September 10; the foundation stone was then brought to Dornach from Munich by Dr. Felix Peipers on September 17. It was kept in the cellar of Haus Hansi where, on September 19, Rudolf Steiner brought two pyrite crystals with instructions for Max Benzinger—one crystal was to be suspended in the center of each dodecahedron. The smaller of the two was to be placed in the large dodecahedron; the larger crystal would be placed in the smaller dodecahedron. To the astonished Ehrenfried Pfeiffer, Rudolf Steiner said, "The pyrite crystals hold the building's two cupolas...,"[31] and he stressed to Benzinger that the foundation stone had to be positioned precisely along an east-west axis.[32]

The time for the foundation stone laying ritual was announced only an hour before the event which finally began at 7:00 p.m. on September 20, 1913, and lasted a total of ninety minutes.[33] Given the short notice, only seventy people knew about it and witnessed it in the evening of what had been a rainy day, on the edge of a trench over which a temporary canopy had been erected.[34] Torches and a bonfire offered scant lighting for the event.

Nine steps led down into the trench that would hold the foundation stone. Standing in the trench, Rudolf Steiner asked the blessings of all of the spiritual hierarchies for what was intended on the Dornach hill and that was now to begin. Turning to the east, south, west, and north, he spoke the words:

> You Seraphim, you Cherubim, you guides of the world, and you who like lightning gather up the sheathes of the Cherubim through the spiritual streams, joining them to the creative being of the world—you lofty Thrones— we call upon you as the protectors of our deed. And you, the spirits of wisdom who are present in humans beings

before they have their being, and you, the keepers of the eternal powers of the world, and you, the shapers of our existence who place the form of all being into the streams of existence, we call upon you to be protectors of our deeds. And you, the spirits of personality in the spiritual stream, and you helpers—Archangels and Angels—who are the messengers of humanity's spiritual life, we call upon all of you to be protectors and guides of this, our deed. We ask you to descend and stand over the human soul we wish to consecrate insofar as it is in our power.[35]

A *consecration of the human being* was to take place—*"insofar as it is in our power;"* consecration of the human being's true nature as the bearer of future evolution. The human soul was to consecrate itself to the work that awaited it, work that it had to complete: "We draw near to this human soul we wish to consecrate to the work that is to serve our age to the degree our knowledge allows."[36]

Rudolf Steiner spoke of the human being, the *anthropos*, not in the sense of the materialism and Darwinism of the time, nor in the sense of genetics and the science of the human body, but as a being descended from the powers of the divine-spiritual hierarchies to whose rank we would ascend in the future as the tenth hierarchy of freedom and love. Rudolf Steiner stressed that this foundation stone had been made according to the "cosmic images of the human soul" and its "emblem"—an emblem of the "striving human soul set as microcosm into the macrocosm," which is revealed in the double dodecahedral nature of the foundation stone's composition. The foundation stone expresses "human beings who wish to seek themselves in the spirit, who wish to feel themselves in the cosmic soul, and who sense themselves in the Cosmic 'I.'" Rudolf Steiner inscribed this human being onto the document placed into the foundation stone not only as a future hope, but also as the problem child of the hierarchies, who knew of the threat confronting the human being.[37]

Standing in the trench, Rudolf Steiner read the Rosicrucian saying inscribed on the foundation stone document: *"Ex deo nascimur / In Christo morimur / Per Spiritum Sanctum reviviscimus,"* which he would translate ten years later as "Out of the divine humanity has its being / In Christ death becomes life / In the cosmic thoughts of the world the soul awakens."[38] He spoke of the fact that the whole "sense" of anthroposophical striving was contained in these Rosicrucian formulations—and it became clear beyond any doubt that Rudolf Steiner's entire intention with this School was bound up with the spiritual intention of the Rosicrucian community in the age of Michael.[39] As the document indicated, the foundation stone laying took place in the year 1880 after the Mystery of Golgotha—a way of counting that Rudolf Steiner had used for the first time eighteen months earlier when noting the 1912 Easter festival in the 1912/13 *Calendar of the Soul*. With Rosicrucian consciousness he had connected it with the true turning point in time that occurred on Golgotha ("1879 after the birth of the 'I' [AD 33]").

Rudolf Steiner was the "spiritual leader" for the act of laying the foundation stone, which was also stated in the document. He not only spoke the words of consecration and placed the document into the foundation stone, but he also proceeded to consecrate the foundation stone itself—striking the small dodecahedron three, five, seven times, and the large dodecahedron twelve times.[40] Rudolf Steiner indicated how the stone would be altered by this ritual process; the emblem would become a sign that afterward would be ensheathed, "outwardly resembling a burial; spiritually, however, a birth":

> The primal image of the human being, the entelechy of the anthropos, is entrusted to the Earth as a potent emblem. The meaning of the Earth's mission is the development of the power of love in the sense of the Christ sacrifice. The final aim of evolution is the transformation of the Earth by the human being so that it becomes a star of love radiating into the cosmos. (Erika von Baravalle)[41]

The dodecahedrons were made of copper, the metal of Venus and of love; the mystery of iron and sulfur in the pyrite crystals was placed into them. Many years later, during his final Mystery course in Torquay in Great Britain, Rudolf Steiner impressively described the cosmic carrying power of iron and sulphur.[42]

More than eleven years after the Dornach foundation stone laying, as he lay in his sick bed, Rudolf Steiner wrote once again about the true meaning of the Earth for the macrocosm (*Was ist die Erde in Wirklichkeit im Makrokosmos?* [In reality, what is the Earth within the macrocosm?]).[43] There he was to explain that the macrocosm is engaged in a death process—it sacrificed its earlier, essential vitality to the human microcosm which was intended to become independent and awakened to its own life. The human "I" could unfold autonomously on the Earth—from being to revelation to independent activity—only if the effects and various influences of the macrocosm receded.[44]

With the rise of the independent microcosm, the macrocosm had to die in a certain respect, i.e., its vitality had to decrease gradually. But then, Rudolf Steiner explained, it would increasingly become a task of the Earth and its kingdoms to return forces to the macrocosm out of themselves. The Earth is no "particle of dust" but, according to Rudolf Steiner, the "embryonic seed" of a cosmos that is newly coming to life and arising.[45] The possible evolution of Earth and the cosmos actually begins with human beings themselves; they have a life-creating principle at their disposal.[46] According to Rudolf Steiner, activating this principle instead of continuing the destructive activity of purely material exploitation and technology is the great "mission of humanity on our planet Earth"[47]—and thus the mission of the Dornach School.

~

In his address in the trench immediately after the laying of the foundation stone, Rudolf Steiner looked back on the turning point of time and called for an inner relationship, an inner connection to its events—*"In this moment let us try to evoke within ourselves the thought of the connection between the human soul and the intention of the turning point of time."*[48] He described the progressive loss of Mystery wisdom and Mystery knowledge just before the time of Christ and the associated separation of human beings from the true "homeland" of their soul-spiritual forces in the cosmos: "Let us try to clarify for ourselves how the connection with divine cosmic existence, with the will, feeling, and divine-spiritual knowledge has faded from human souls."[49]

While developing their personality, human beings had to free themselves from their true home, or macrocosmic affiliation. Henceforth, they lived through their own powers in bodies that gave them their earthly self-awareness, or "earthly 'I.'"[50] This process was necessary and irreversible in the history of consciousness. According to Rudolf Steiner, in the centuries before the turning point of time, human beings arrived at a critical point or decisive crisis that could be overcome in a fully living way only through the Mystery of the Christ's Incarnation and through the process of death and resurrection on Golgotha.

> Humanity had earlier reached an endpoint in its striving for personality. When the ancient legacy of the divine teachers at the very beginning of Earth evolution had withered away in the fullness of this Earth personality there appeared in the east the cosmic words, *"In the beginning was the Word/ And the Word was with God/ And the Word was a God." And the Word appeared to human souls and spoke to them: Fulfill the evolution of the Earth through the meaning of the Earth!—Now the Word itself has passed into the Earth's aura; the spiritual aura of the Earth has absorbed the Word into itself.*[51]

Seen from this perspective the events at the Jordan and on Golgotha are the laying of a foundation stone as well.[52] With the incarnation of Christ in an earthly body and with the events on Golgotha—the destiny of Christ's body and blood (and their union with the Earth's organism and the aura of the Earth)[53]—the tangible resurrection of the Earth and humanity began; the seed of "new life" was planted in the old life's crisis of dying.

The substance of this ascending human evolution began to have an effect in those human souls who had joined with the Christ and His work, His "impulse" during His three years on Earth and after His death. Through what took place during the three years—the Baptism in the Jordan and its "fulfillment" on Golgotha[54]—Christ became a human being and from then on He was united with the fate of humanity on Earth. The connection with Him as the "Cosmic Word" and "true 'I'" that came from cosmic heights and united itself with the destiny of Earth made it possible for the human soul to connect with the cosmos once more. According to Rudolf Steiner, Christ changed the human situation on Earth through His deed; He made it possible for those who wish to follow Him to overcome not only the "sickness of sin" but also to overcome the constellation of forces that lay at the root of that sickness, forces that had separated humanity from the true home of its being in favor of a forced incarnation, a fall into earthly matter. The mantric lamentation to the gods in the pre-Christian initiation schools that knew about the situation of the (hyper)incarnated spirit on Earth was turned by Jesus Christ during His physical passage through the turning point of time into the Lord's Prayer that He taught to His esoteric students:

> AUM, Amen!
> The evils hold sway,
> Witness of egoity becoming free,
> Selfhood guilt through others incurred,
> Experience in your daily bread,
> Where the will of the heavens holds no sway
> Since the human being severed himself
>   from your kingdom
> And forgot your names,
> You fathers in heaven.[55]

> Father, You Who were, are, and will be in the inmost
>   being of us all!
> Your being is glorified and praised in us all.
> May Your kingdom be broadened through our deeds
>   and the conduct of our life.
> We do Your will in the deeds of our life as You,
>   O Father, have placed it into our inmost souls.

"The evils hold sway..."

>   Throughout the changing circumstances of our life
>   You offer us in fullness the nourishment of the
>   spirit, the bread of life.
>   May our mercy for others be compensation for the
>   sins enacted against our being.
>   You do not let the tempter work in us beyond the limits of our power since there can be no temptation
>   in Your being; for the tempter is only illusion and
>   deception out of which You, O Father, will surely
>   lead us through the light of Your knowledge.
>   May Your power and glory work in us throughout the
>   cycles of the cycles of time.[56]

~

Rudolf Steiner and the anthroposophical movement worked toward this esoteric Christ-impulse—and the "School for Spiritual Science" was to remain on this path in the "House of the Word" whose foundation stone was laid on September 20, 1913, in Dornach. In founding the Dornach School Rudolf Steiner strove from the outset for a renewal of the fields of civilized life in the context of an active Christ-impulse, a renewal based on the strength of esoteric professional communities.[57] A "thoroughly Christianized" thinking was to be introduced into the different areas of life and realms of knowledge, a thinking that was in a position to regain access to true "cosmic thoughts," the intentions of creation—to the creative, cosmically determined or jointly determined systems, laws, and forces in the realm of nature and the human being. The Dornach School was meant to reawaken human and Christ consciousness[58] through an active form of spiritual Rosicrucianism in the Michael Age,[59] and practice them in a tangible way. As Rudolf Steiner later emphasized in his address given on the evening of September 19, 1914, as preparation for the first anniversary of the foundation stone laying, this was to be accomplished through an inner connection to what began at the turning point in time—the evolution of the Earth to become Sun, its macrocosmic "illumination," its healing and preparation for the future—i.e., its preparation as a "place in the cosmos where holy, spiritual, Christ-sunlight will be radiant" in the future.[60] The "Johannes Building," as the center for the esoteric Christianity of the modern age, was to serve the further development of science, art, and religion—in a transformed thinking, feeling, and willing that flowed into beauty. The poet Christian Morgenstern wrote in regard to Rudolf Steiner and Anthroposophy:

> Your work leads to beauty;
> for at last beauty streams in
> through all revelation
> that brings it to us.
> From human afflictions
> you release ascendant feeling
> to ever-higher harmonies until—
> united with the accord
> of the infinite heralds of GOD
> and HIS incomprehensible glory—
> it resonates in the loving light
> of bliss...
> from beauty comes
> and to beauty leads
> your work.[61]

Rudolf Steiner spoke of the Dornach building as a "holy matter" for the anthroposophical community, and at the foundation stone laying he made it clear that the ritual act was binding; this binding quality included those people who participated in the foundation stone laying and considered themselves part of the Anthroposophical Society and movement. "Let us understand that for our soul this deed signifies a vow in a certain sense."[62] According to Rudolf Steiner, the work now begun together represented a vow (or rather the people who wished to support it and be responsible for it had "taken a vow") to the being of the "Christ impulse," to the ongoing historical destiny of the world, and to the purpose of the Mystery of Golgotha. "Let us understand that today...we are taking a vow to this spiritual evolutionary stream of humanity that we have recognized as right."[63]

In his later addresses, Rudolf Steiner repeatedly recalled this concrete promise of fidelity, a promise made—at least indirectly—by those who of their own free will had chosen to be eyewitnesses to what took place on September 20, 1913. This emerged in a renewal of that promise, the renewal of the truly consummated "vow." In his lecture on September 20, 1916, commemorating the laying of the foundation stone, he said: "And so today, as we have tried to look back at the impulses that filled our souls three years ago, we can only renew our most inward pledge to will to remain *true to this impulse.*"[64] A little more than ten years after the laying of the foundation stone, Rudolf Steiner gave a lecture on December 31, 1923, the first anniversary of the fire that completely destroyed the building begun in 1913. The audience stood to greet him and during the course of his remarks he asked those present to stand once again:

> My dear friends, you have received me by rising in memory of the old Goetheanum. You live in the memory of this old Goetheanum. Let us rise now as a sign that we are taking a vow to continue working in the spirit of the

Goetheanum with the best forces we can find within the image of our human nature. Yes, so be it. Amen.

Thus, in accord with the will that unites our human souls with the souls of the gods to whom we wish to remain true in the spirit, we will to keep it [the vow] as long as we are able, my dear friends; we will to do so based on the spirit in which we sought this loyalty to them at a special moment in our lives—the moment when we sought the Spiritual Science of the Goetheanum. *And may we understand how to continue this loyalty.*[65]

When Rudolf Steiner had announced the "Endowment for a Theosophical Art and Way of Life" in Berlin at the end of 1911 he had already spoken to a certain extent about these spiritual-moral prerequisites for the Dornach building and the School for Spiritual Science intended with it—almost two years before the first foundation stone laying, and yet with a spiritual connection to it. There were no "honors," no "high ranks" connected with the responsibilities and leadership tasks of this contemporary Rosicrucian impulse, only duties, only a genuine capacity for a selflessness based in knowledge that excludes or overcomes "everything, everything personal"[66]—with the inner mood of an approaching cultural epoch that must in the present time be prepared and take its first steps.

The placement of the copper dodecahedron into the earth on September 20, 1913, was obviously a physical deed, but Rudolf Steiner also spoke about what he called the "spiritual portion [of the foundation stone] provided by the power of the human soul," which must be added to the physical placement of the foundation stone for it to be complete, effective, and enduring. "With humility, devotion, and a willingness to sacrifice we seek to guide our souls upward to the great plans, the great goals of human endeavor on the Earth."[67] Not only was the idealized knowledge of these "plans" and "goals" necessary—plans and goals Rudolf Steiner had spoken about for years in his anthroposophical lectures—but an inner attitude of "humility, devotion, and a willingness to sacrifice" were also required. Without them, shared work on the common goals was impossible. From his coworkers Rudolf Steiner expected selflessness and an absolute readiness to work for the "holy matter" of the building; he also expected a social or "brotherly" attitude to be taken into one's heart or—if necessary—"forced" into it "so that each person thinks the best of everyone else."[68] Rudolf Steiner called on his anthroposophical friends to look away from "everything petty in life," to concentrate on the essential, and to build the effective working community required for the accomplishment of future tasks. He spoke about the individual and community courage that was needed, about the "courage of one's convictions" and the courage for loyalty that would be required in the future.

Rudolf Steiner no doubt knew the difficult times that Anthroposophy and the Dornach School project would face—and the degree to which they stood diametrically opposed to the powerfully prevalent and increasingly influential current of the time. As he described in many anthroposophical lectures, the confrontation with the forces of evil is the pivotal challenge of the modern cultural epoch—both in the area of knowledge *and* of action. Several years after the laying of the foundation stone, Rudolf Steiner spoke in Dornach about the "fully conscious battle against the evil emerging in the evolution of humanity."[69] He already knew about this task in 1913 and (to the likely astonishment of those present) gave it a central place in laying the foundation stone ("*The evils hold sway...*").

Moreover, Rudolf Steiner was clear that, in this regard, the question of community would also be a decisive factor in the future. On the other hand, isolated individuals would be entirely unable to confront evil successfully, a confrontation that was part of the occult task for the Dornach School. Much more urgently needed in this realm was the united work of the Anthroposophical Society. In the future, the opposing forces of destruction would no doubt attempt to break into the circle of this community and exploit the weaknesses in the souls of individuals there. Between 1910 and 1913, Rudolf Steiner had had all four of his Mystery dramas performed in the presence of (and by) the members of the Anthroposophical Society. In these dramas he portrayed the intrusion of these forces of seduction and alienation into the untransformed soul regions of spiritually seeking people. "Rosicrucianism has in itself the impulses that should be used to counter the demons," said Rudolf Steiner.[70] He knew well the wakefulness that the community would have to cultivate in the future in order to conduct this dangerous battle and survive it successfully. By including the "inverted Lord's Prayer" from the *Fifth Gospel* in his address at the laying of the foundation stone and reciting it twice (as the central mantra of September 20, 1913), Rudolf Steiner indirectly made it clear that its content had in no way been fully replaced or made irrelevant by the Mystery of Golgotha. Why else would he have spoken these ancient verses during the consecration of a place that was dedicated unmistakably to the future, not to the pre-Christian past? Within Jesus Christ' esoteric group of disciples and through the effect He had on them, He had initiated a way of development that entered the world after Whitsun and ran counter to these forces of evil. However, almost two thousand years later the "evils" and the forces of evil still (or in an even more intense way) held sway within the depths of the human soul. The egocentric forces of the culture of personality, "egoity becoming free," and "selfhood guilt through others incurred" were in no way transcended in civilization at large *nor* in the circle of anthroposophists—just the opposite. In addition, humanity continued as before to forget divine-spiritual intentions and forces, "heaven's will," in the practical matters of life. And this was true in Dornach—the predestined Mystery site—as well. The human being forgot not only the "name" of the lofty hierarchies but, for the most part, acted as though they did not exist. When Rudolf Steiner spoke the inverted Lord's Prayer in mantric form, he called these connections to consciousness in an intense way; at the same time, he prepared a form for creating a community at this abyss— one based on more than a shared ideal of the good. From this perspective, the Mystery deed of the Dornach foundation stone laying differentiated itself explicitly from other beginnings. It was not carried out exclusively through the invocation of truth, goodness, and beauty—positive ideals—but through coming face to face with evil as well. Thus, it was a ritual act of the modern age.

To ensure the continuation of these difficult tasks Rudolf Steiner looked to the development of the individual and the community within and through the building, a *"true building"* that he said would become a "cornerstone" for further development. Rudolf Steiner looked to the building's forms—forms that called forth self-knowledge in every detail—to provide help for the schooling that would take place there; at the same time these forms made central elements of the future visible in an artistic way. Rudolf Steiner had already spoken about the planned interior of the building at the first general meeting of the Johannes Building Association held in Berlin at the end of 1911—close to the time the "Endowment for a Theosophical Art and Way of Life" was announced. He described it as an interior that "denies itself, that no longer develops any egotism of space, so that everything it offers in the way of colors and forms will be there selflessly in order to allow the cosmos to enter."[71] In this way, the building's forms and colors—even the whole artistic shaping of what was being planned in Dornach including the central sculpture, *The Representative of Humanity*—were intended to help the individual and the community gather their forces and bring these forces to bear on behalf of the task for civilization.[72] In his address immediately following the foundation stone laying Rudolf Steiner spoke of a "great spiritual battle" that must be fought "illumined through and through by the fire of love."[73] A year and a half later, at Whitsun 1915, he said during another address in Dornach:

> Not with pride but in all humility we will feel what is to be carried into the world through Spiritual Science. We feel it especially in our difficult age, in our age that poses so many questions to our feelings, questions that can only be answered when Spiritual Science can make its true worth known. I have no wish to evoke a sense of arrogance in anyone, but I would like to repeat a statement once made during a great event when mention was made of what was to happen through those souls that had taken up a task they were to carry out. These souls were told—not to arouse their pride, but in an appeal to their humility—"You are the salt of the earth."[74]

In a ritual act on September 20, 1913, Rudolf Steiner committed the copper double dodecahedron foundation stone with its suspended pyrite crystals to the earth in Dornach—encased in a protective concrete covering. The extent to which the anthroposophical community would be able—if at all—to carry this foundation stone in itself, in its very being, remained for the time being an open question. As Rudolf Steiner said in his commemorative address on the first anniversary of the foundation stone laying, it depended mainly on the "fundamental attitude" of individual anthroposophists and their esoteric community, an attitude that had to live in the heart as a "spiritual foundation stone" if they were to accomplish the goal intended in Dornach, or even come close to it. ("That, my dear friends, must also be a foundation stone, one we wish to lay in our hearts, and upon which we intend to build the invisible building symbolized by the outwardly visible one.")[75] In an expression Rudolf Steiner used at the beginning of the foundation stone laying in 1913, this deed and what was experienced through it should be "inscribed" into the participants. ("Try to inscribe in your souls the greatness of the moment we are undergoing this evening.")

There can be no doubt that he saw a connection between the "inscription" that was to be accomplished there and the spiritual heart organ—the central destiny organ of human existence that can take into itself actions and their intentions ("inscribe"), relate them to the karmic past and transform them into the future.[76] As Rudolf Steiner indicated, it is in the heart of anthroposophists that their special destiny lies hidden, a destiny to which they must awaken. One of the preeminent moments—or at least "chances"—for this awakening took place with the foundation stone laying for the Dornach building and its school—as it was happening and in memory.

2

The Supersensible Michael Community

and the Destiny of the Anthroposophical Society

Lecture in Dornach, February 21, 2013

"The most intensive preparation of the Michael impulses is unfolding in the supersensible realm, impulses that were to a certain extent brought from Heaven to the Earth during this time, our time." [77]

The Michael Community in Battle

The Supersensible Michael Community

Dear friends,

If we ask about the history and destiny of the Anthroposophical Society and movement, it is necessary—as Rudolf Steiner taught—to take supersensible facts into account in a "thoroughgoing mood of knowledge."[78] We typically write biographies and historical documentation concerning the anthroposophical community, but in the process we ought be consciously aware that we are not presenting its essential element fully. For the community of people around Rudolf Steiner, "connecting" to "what took place in previous centuries" was only possible in a very limited way. The impulses of knowledge and the activity of this community did not arise (or did not primarily arise) within earthly relationships, in the "context" of time and space—although, as Rudolf Steiner emphasized, that context must be "known": "With the consciousness of the present time we must [however] connect with what played out in the supersensible realm during the last centuries."[79]

Following the Christmas Conference 1923/24, Rudolf Steiner wanted these relationships—at long last—to be considered, understood, and internalized. He spoke repeatedly about the necessary "esoteric quality" that must henceforth run through the anthroposophical movement. ("Only then will it be possible to give the anthroposophical movement its true spiritual content."[80]) In the summer of 1924, following a long and systematic preparation, he began to give his lectures on karmic relationships, and for the first time he disclosed details of the developmental steps taken in the supersensible realm by the anthroposophical community. He did so in the hope that the profound character of these details would be understood and taken up through acts of will during those embattled times. He spoke about the spiritual experiences of specific groups of people in the spiritual world before birth, about a step-by-step instruction in the Michael community based in a particular social relationship with precisely delineated tasks and aims. "In this way souls were prepared who then descended to the physical world where they were to maintain the urgent intention that underlies all these preparations: to move toward what would be active on Earth as Anthroposophy."[81] In this sense, then, Rudolf Steiner's karma lectures were not only concerned with the destinies of individual world historical figures but primarily with communities—and especially the community that stood in close connection with Michael, the community critically decisive for Dornach and the School for Spiritual Science. This community was created in the supersensible realm and in the realm of the unborn—in that world where souls are genuinely able to coexist in the being of the other—i.e., they are able to share with others in a way and with an intensity not normally achieved on Earth. The ability to imitate in early childhood is a last—but significant—remnant of this pre-earthly existence.[82] In his remarks, Rudolf Steiner also explains the degree to which the Michael community has a certain relationship with the spiritual Sun and the heart organ: over and over again, he sought to draw the attention of his anthroposophical friends to the secrets of this heart organ.

In his karma lectures, Rudolf Steiner essentially describes *three* cosmic steps of development taken by the Michael community since the turning point of time—and he stressed that the first two occurred in the sphere of the spiritual Sun.

According to Rudolf Steiner, Michael (together with his "radiant garment"—the spiritual host of angels and archangels belonging with him—and accompanied as well by innumerable human souls) had observed the Mystery of Golgotha from the vantage point of the "consecrated Sun sphere"; even earlier he had seen the Christ spirit turning toward the Earth. These human souls, remarked Rudolf Steiner, served the angels and were thus chosen by destiny ("predisposed") to find Anthroposophy in later eras and have the capacity to represent it on Earth.

As Rudolf Steiner depicts it, Christ's departure from the Sun sphere, his actual "leaving," was a mighty, deeply moving, and shocking experience for the community around Michael, the leading Sun archangel.

> It is...one of the events we must look at: those human souls closely connected with the anthroposophical movement carry in them that scene: "We are united with Michael on the Sun; the Christ—who, until then, had sent his impulses to the Earth from the Sun—now goes forth from the Sun to unite himself with the evolution of the Earth!"[83]

Rudolf Steiner does not indicate in detail when—according to the calculation of time on Earth—this "scene" occurred, a scene that included not only the beginnings of Christ's separation from the Sun but also the whole process of His turning to the Earth and its culmination in the Mystery of Golgotha.[84] It became clear to the Michael community that the Christ joined his destiny with the Earth and with an endangered humanity. He carried the forces of the Sun to the Earth in sacrifice, or at least prepared the way for them—and thus made possible the first elements of what would one day be manifested when the Earth becomes Sun:[85]

> Light is love... Sun-weaving
> love-radiance of a world
> of creative beings—
> which throughout unimaginable ages
> holds us to its heart
> and gave to us at last
> its loftiest spirit in a
> human sheathe for three
> years; there He came into His
> Father's birthright—now the inmost
> heavenly fire of the Earth:
> so it, too, will one day become Sun.[86]

As Rudolf Steiner explained, Michael had witnessed the turning of the Christ to the Earth, His "departure" from the Sun, and His connection with the destiny of humanity. This was the sign for Michael that he was now gradually to transfer to the Earth the "cosmic thoughts" of the "cosmic intelligence" he had "administered" for humanity as a servant of the divine-spiritual forces in cosmic heights.[87] Until the turning point in time, these cosmic thoughts had primarily been active in the sacred realm of the Mystery sites—as a "heavenly inspiration" for human thinking— and from there they had worked to support the general development of civilization. According to Rudolf Steiner, the Christ had sent His impulses to the Earth from the Sun in pre-Christian times —as did Michael.

> [Michael] was preeminent among the archangels—insofar as they populate the Sun. He was that spirit who not only sent the physical-etheric rays from the Sun but also the one who sent inspiring intellectuality to the Earth within those physical-etheric rays of Sun.[88]

The spiritual thinking of leading groups of people had been cosmically inspired by Michael after they had first undergone a schooling that allowed them to develop a spiritual sensitivity for what "cosmic-Being-light" and "spiritual cosmic thoughts" actually were and what they required of human beings.

On the other hand, *before* the turning point in time Michael had already worked to prepare the way in a certain sense so that the forces of cosmic intelligence could gradually enter into the inmost space of the human soul on Earth in the future. According to Rudolf Steiner, during the time of Michael's earlier regency (as the "time spirit" prior to the Mystery of Golgotha), it was Aristotle who primarily represented an "inwardly active intelligence" during the fourth century BC. This was a step away from the realm of the Mysteries that marked the onset of the separation of earthly intelligence from the cosmic intelligence—in and of itself an expression of the active Michael impulse.[89]

Through his participation in and later comprehension of Christ's path to Earth, Michael knew that the establishment of a purely earthly intelligence separated from its cosmic source was a future necessity for all of human evolution. As the Sun archangel, he experienced the turning point in time—together with his hierarchic "hosts" but also with excarnated human individualities like Plato, Aristotle, and Alexander the Great who were among the principal members of the Michael community. According to Rudolf Steiner, only after this experience was Michael able to reach a decision to release the intelligence completely and allow it to flow down as "sacred rain" onto the Earth, which the Christ had chosen as the place where he would assume human form. And it would be in the surroundings of this Earth that He would reside in a tangible way after the Mystery of Golgotha.

> GRASP what reveals itself to you!
> Sense your ascent to the Sun!
> Sense what creator-bliss
> Fills every being there.
> Climb then these spirit-steps
> Up to the highest host!
> And then finally perceive Him
> The master of all these spirits!
> And come then, descend with Him!
> Among people and demons
> Come with Him, indwell the body,
> Yielded to Him by a man devout.
> Can a heart grasp the sacrifices' greatness?
> Can a spirit measure this sacrifice in full?
> How a God relinquishes heaven's glory
> For human need and nakedness![90]

~

The process of transferring the forces of intelligence from the cosmic heights into earthly conditions lasted a long time—condensing into human individuality the intelligence that had been active throughout the cosmos. As described by Rudolf Steiner, the "rays" of intelligence administered by Michael did not completely arrive on the Earth until the ninth century AD. Then the first theologians and philosophers (like Duns Scotus Erigena but also Harun al Raschid) appeared, "independent thinkers" in the true sense who were no longer subject to cosmically inspired ways of thinking.

> With the ninth century...personal individual intelligence lit up in human souls. The human being had the feeling: I *form* thoughts. And this forming of thoughts was paramount in the life of the soul so that those who were thinking saw the essence of the human soul in its intelligent behavior.[91]...

Within the choir of archangels in the region of the Sun, and from out of Michael's being sounded the mighty word: "What had been the power of my realm, what had been administered here by me is no longer here; it must continue to stream, to surge, to pour forth on the Earth there below."[92]

Because Michael was unable to intervene in the destiny of the Earth at that time, this process eventually led to new incarnation tasks for human souls who were members of the Michael community and had a particular responsibility within it. As Rudolf Steiner emphasized, those individualities were among the ones who now incarnated; they had belonged to the Platonic stage of the previous, pre-Christian Michael age—and thus had immediately preceded the Aristotelian turn in the nature of thinking (toward an "inner activity of intelligence"). They created on the Earth the college of teachers at the School of Chartres—that significant and widely influential school. In its grandiose instruction and schooling lived not just imaginative images of the evolution of the world and of humanity and a thoroughly Christianized Platonism—a Christianity that stood in the effulgence of the Old Mysteries; there was also an association with an intelligence that still revealed qualities of its cosmic origin, that knew about this cosmic dimension.

> Powerful teachers! This was the way they spoke in the School of Chartres—as if Plato, interpreting Christianity, was personally active among these spirits. They taught the spiritual content of Christianity.... They did not teach with the intellect. They taught entirely in mighty images they unfurled before their audience—images that vividly set forth the spiritual content of Christianity.[93]

On the other hand, during the period immediately following, individuals with a leaning toward Aristotelianism—among them, the individuality of Aristotle himself—created the core of the Dominican community that had been founded as a mendicant order. Soon, the members who were influential in setting its tone and were endowed with brilliant intellectual capacities found it possible to expand into the universities and contribute formatively to the public intellectual life of their time. This was of paramount importance because one of the primary tasks of the Michael community was to care for the "administration" of the intellectual life on Earth from that time forward.

The "Michaelites" of the Dominican Order—like their predecessors and spiritual friends, the Platonists—had observed the Mystery of Golgotha from the Sun sphere together with Michael. They stood for the spiritual "realism" of the life of thought, i.e., campaigned for recognition of the fact that ideas were real beings and not abstract constructs about human topics that had been turned into language. "One must say the following about...the teaching of Aristotle: the thought content...is the nature or the being of the thing in question" (Thomas Aquinas).[94] "The realistic scholastics ascribed spiritual reality to what the human being grasped by means of thoughts—a spiritual-intellectual reality. It is a thin spirituality that could be rescued there—but it is spirituality."[95] Rudolf Steiner emphasized that "[all] of scholasticism is a human struggle for clarity about the intelligence that was streaming in...the light-filled, the spiritual intelligence."[96] He also indicated that it was the task of the Dominicans to develop intelligence further so that during the time of Michael's renewed earthly activity in the future—the next Michael epoch—he would be able to reunite himself with it. And this would occur in and by means of the human being.[97]

The Supersensible Michael Community

The Platonists of the School of Chartres and the Dominicans around Albertus Magnus and Thomas Aquinas who followed and were inspired by them worked to assure that consciousness of the Mysteries of human intelligence and its cosmic origin would not be lost—and a concept of the "I" could gradually develop. It would be a concept that was to join the activity and autonomy of the thinking human spirit to participation in an overarching lawfulness—that is, a concept of the "I" with a cosmic orientation. The Platonic and Aristotelian souls thus prepared the way for Michael. They knew of his future involvement with the Earth and worked together for that future, although each had their own emphasis.[98] Both groups belonged to the core of the Michael community and stood in Michael's service. According to Rudolf Steiner they looked to the last third of the nineteenth century when the principal archangel of the Sun would once again become the determining time spirit—at the rank of an archai—and would collaborate significantly in shaping the development of civilization. In order to prepare this future effectively, the Platonists of Chartres and the leading individualities of the Dominican Order had arranged their successive incarnations with one another in the sphere before birth under the guidance of Michael.

> It was possible to see Anthroposophy arising in a living way like a being that had to be born, but—as though in a mother's womb—it rested within what had come to the Earth in the first centuries of Christianity, what had been prepared by the School of Chartres, and what then had been carried forward in the supersensible realm in collaboration with what continued on the Earth as the defense of Christianity, a defense colored by Aristotelianism.[99]

Rudolf Steiner goes on to describe how the next significant cosmic step in the development of the Michael community again occurred in the *Sun sphere* during the existence between death and a new birth. Among the periods of transition for the human individuality after death, the one in the Sun sphere not only lasts longest but is also decisively connected with the creation of future destiny. Essential steps toward the spiritual conception of the next earthly life in a physical body along with the destiny constellation, the destiny affirmation, are configured in the Sun sphere in cooperation with the first hierarchy.[100] It is a sphere of pure goodness and love in which the purest intentions of the individual and the community come to fruition.[101]

This cosmic realm had been chosen in pre-Christian times by the Christ-being Himself as the central place for His "sojourn" and, from the beginning of the fifteenth century onward, it was here that Michael taught his pupils as the "consciousness soul" age was dawning on the Earth and the Rosicrucian community was being formed. Materialism was growing step by step in the development of human civilization, and the next possibility for Michael to work actively on the Earth was still centuries away. Freed from his earlier tasks—the "administration" of cosmic intelligence—and largely without an opportunity to intervene in the destinies of incarnated human beings, Michael held his school "in heavenly solitude."[102] Just as it had been at the turning point in time, "his" hosts were once again assembled around him, beings from the third hierarchy ("who were part of the Michael stream"), a "large number of elemental beings," but also individualities who were especially connected with Michael—among them the teachers of Chartres (like Alanus ab Insulis or Bernardus Silvestris) and the spiritual leaders of the Dominican Order. There were also many, many other souls "whose inner quality of soul yearned for a renewal of Christianity."[103] The next step in forming a spiritual community was taken in this cosmic space of an all-embracing love—and it happened in the course of a schooling that lasted almost three centuries. According to Rudolf Steiner, Michael taught anthroposophical and cosmosophical relationships, human and cosmic secrets, "wonderful grandiose teachings" in "great, mighty cosmic words" that entered into the community as "inner teachings of the heart." He brought to life for the community "what had once lived in the Sun Mysteries as Michael wisdom." However, in a certain respect he also depicted the development of culture and consciousness in which the human souls around him had themselves taken part:

> What was summarized there in a grandiose way was the continuation of Platonism in an Aristotelianism brought over into Asia and down into Egypt by Alexander the Great. There was an explanation of how the old spirituality still lived in it.[104]

Rudolf Steiner goes on to say that Michael offered a comprehensive panorama in which he not only summarized the old initiation wisdom, the "great teachings of the old Mysteries," but also prepared for the transition of this wisdom to the consciousness of intelligence or the "consciousness soul." The content of what had been promulgated through these old or ancient teachings needed to reflect the fact that what had been cosmic intelligence in the previous centuries had now become earthly—and that intelligence had to become increasingly accessible to the activity of individual human intelligence.

> Everything taught there [in the Michael School] was taught from the standpoint that what had been appropriate for Michael now had to be developed in a different

way in the evolution of humanity below, now had to be developed through the individual intelligence of the human soul.[105]

In this sense, the instruction that took place for three centuries in the cosmic Sun sphere was not only recapitulation but also a preparation of destiny for the future—it was not just a review; it was also a "mighty panorama of what was to take place." According to Rudolf Steiner, Michael taught "what is to happen when the new Michael age begins." His coworkers and pupils received "riveting admonitions" so that "[in the future] those gathered around Michael might plunge into the Michael stream, take up its impulses, so that the intelligence would once again be united with the Michael-being." Thus a shared future destiny was prepared—in a way, as Rudolf Steiner emphasized, that introduced something new into the evolution of the Earth and humanity.[106]

During the time of the "Michael School" the members of the "Michael community" followed further developments on the Earth intensively. They were able to experience from the cosmic sphere of the Sun how the first hierarchy fully incorporated the earthly powers of intelligence into the human nerve-sense system in the first third of the fifteenth century (i.e., right at the beginning of the community's instruction in the Mysteries). The Michael community observed the drama of these events on the Earth in an elemental way—they saw the Earth "ringed about with mighty lightning and thunder,"[107] and experienced the complete reshaping of the human being. The first hierarchy of the cosmos (the Seraphim, Cherubim, and Thrones) penetrated to the inmost part of the human head and organized the possibility of intelligent "head thinking"—a purely cognitive thought process that was mirrored in the nerve-sense and was intrinsically abstract. When independent thinkers during the centuries just before the age of the consciousness soul thought, the rest of their soul forces participated in their thinking; the act of the first hierarchy now gave them—for the first time—the organic-physiologic possibility for forming pure head thinking without the participation of the other soul forces. This created an integral, even formative, element of the new age dawning in the history of consciousness and the evolution of civilization.

Moreover, during the centuries of their instruction in the Sun sphere the members of the "Michael School" experienced what unfolded in response to their Mystery schooling and preparation for the future as the reaction on Earth turned to resistance and took form. According to Rudolf Steiner, as the Michael School and its schooling "expanded mightily in the Sun sphere" a concentrated opposition was stirring in the ahrimanic power on Earth—"[the Michael School] was something tremendous, something that deeply dismayed the ahrimanic demons on the Earth during the fifteenth, sixteenth, seventeenth centuries and into the eighteenth century, and it brought them into a terrible state of agitation."[108] In the end, Ahriman established a school in opposition to the Michael School; its work did not begin in the cosmic heights of the Sun but in the depths of the planet Earth—as something "subterranean." From below, it sent its forces up into the development of humanity. Rudolf Steiner described—or outlined—its "impulses rising up in a demonic spiritual haze, impulses that encouraged the development of the art of printing (among other things) in the evolution of civilization." The "mechanically fixed" letter became an instrument for Ahriman to use against Michael. Michael himself sought at the beginning of the nineteenth century to reunite the head intelligence of the human being with heart processes, thus with the whole human being. Ahriman opposed this developmental direction with all his might. He wanted to "absorb" the intelligence that had fallen to the Earth (i.e., had been released from the cosmos), to bind it to himself, and thereby "wrest it away" from Michael forever.

> At the same time the cosmic intelligence was descending from the cosmos to the Earth, the aspirations of the ahrimanic forces to wrest this cosmic intelligence (to the extent it had become earthly) from Michael continued to grow; thus free from Michael, it would have validity only on Earth. That has been the great crisis from the beginning of the fifteenth century until today; we are still involved in this crisis, the crisis expressed as the battle of Ahriman against Michael: Ahriman, who used every means at his disposal to vie with Michael for the intelligence that had now become earthly...[109]

Rudolf Steiner spoke of a mighty battle that began in the fifteenth century and continued to grow and intensify before the eyes of the Michael pupils. ("Among other things, being an anthroposophist means understanding this battle—at least to some extent."[110]) At the time of their Sun period, Michael's pupils and coworkers had the task of perceiving—preliminarily, in any case—the configuration and drama of this battle so that later they would be able to take an active part in support of Michael. Rudolf Steiner spoke about this situation that was occurring shortly after leading members of the Michael community began to incarnate during the latter part of the nineteenth century:

Mighty phenomena took place behind a veil, all of them grouped around a spiritual being whom we designate as Michael. Powerful followers of Michael were present, human souls who were not in a physical body at that time but were between death and a new birth; however, powerful demonic forces under the influence of Ahriman were also present, forces that revolted against what was to enter the world through Michael.[111]

Rudolf Steiner relates that the passage of the Michael pupils through the Sun sphere in the three centuries after the onset of the consciousness soul age strengthened the determination in each to move ahead in the direction described and with an existential commitment. The "yearning for Anthroposophy" and the readiness at the end of the nineteenth century to commit to what could enter civilization from then on as Anthroposophy arose at this time; it was, in fact, a pivotal result of the instruction they had passed through. ("Those who have a real yearning for Anthroposophy are...experiencing today in their souls the aftereffects of the fact that they were in the circle surrounding Michael at that time and had taken up the heavenly Anthroposophy that preceded the earthly Anthroposophy. The teachings of Michael at that time were such that they prepared what was intended to become Anthroposophy on Earth."[112])

The next incarnation for the leading Platonic and Aristotelian souls of the Michael stream was to take place gradually after the dawn of the Michael Age in late autumn 1879—at the end of the nineteenth century and during the twentieth century. However, during the first half of the nineteenth century—as they approached the Earth (once again) after having passed through the Michael School in the period between the fifteenth and the eighteenth centuries—the Michael community once again underwent a particular intensification in its situation. The result was an effective, sustainable concentration of its forces of will and forces for the future. Rudolf Steiner spoke of a "great overarching event in the spiritual world" that took place "immediately bordering the physical world"—very likely in the Moon sphere. Rudolf Steiner describes how "all" Platonists and Aristotelians were brought together once again for this "event" while on their way to a new birth.[113] What took place in their presence and with them was a "heavenly cultus" in which the content taught in the previous Michael School (the school they had passed through in the centuries before) took on imaginative, cultic form and was actually celebrated in a ritual:

> At the end of the eighteenth and the beginning of the nineteenth centuries a supersensible event was actually hovering quite close to the physical-sensory world—immediately bordering it; of course, this is meant qualitatively. This event presents supersensible cultic acts, a mighty unfolding in pictures of spiritual life, the beings of the cosmos, the beings of the hierarchies, all in connection with the great etheric activities of the cosmos and with human activities on the Earth.[114]

Rudolf Steiner spoke about a great "cosmic-spiritual celebration" held over the course of a few decades; within this "celebration" "mighty imaginations" were actually enacted by the community—no longer by Michael himself, but under the leadership of his outstanding pupils who now "developed" in mighty pictures what they had acquired during the preceding centuries in the supersensible Michael School. The best teachers from the School of Chartres (around Alanus ab Insulis) and the foremost individualities from the Dominican community were active at the "forefront" of the "event"—either performing these acts or leading them. Performed and participated in, the cultus deepened not only the experience of its contents (the "mighty unfolding in pictures of spiritual life, the beings of the cosmos, the beings of the hierarchies"), but strengthened the community as such—and thereby worked into the future to build and shape its social life.

> Those who today feel the yearning *to unite in the Anthroposophical Society* were together in supersensible regions at the beginning of the nineteenth century in order to enact that mighty imaginative cultus.[115]

Rudolf Steiner emphasizes that the "supersensible content of the cultus" consisted of "communally woven cosmic imaginations."[116] In a certain way, they were the product of actual cooperation, an actual "collaboration" of those souls that belonged to the Michael community and were now about to incarnate in the course of the nineteenth and twentieth centuries.

Rudolf Steiner did not give a detailed description in his lectures of the "imaginative cultus" taking place in the sphere bordering the Earth. However, his many remarks make evident that over the course of a half-century (from the end of the eighteenth to the middle of the nineteenth century) the souls in the Michael community were once again united and strengthened in their connection (although not all of them had been present on the Earth at the same time previously). They also received a powerful impulse to incarnate into the Michael–Ahriman battle over Anthroposophy and the future of the human being and to be active in that battle as a *community*. As Rudolf

Steiner repeatedly indicated, materialism on Earth reached its zenith in the first four decades of the nineteenth century. ("The researcher of the spirit can even state precisely that the year materialism reached its high point was around 1840–41."[117])

However, the Michael cultus was taking place parallel to this, and Michael pupils found in it the power and assurance they needed in order to meet the coming challenges. In his lecture on July 18, 1924, Rudolf Steiner indirectly indicated that he himself had been an active participant in this cultus, and that he was well acquainted with the individualities of the people who would become active with him in building and developing the Anthroposophical Society during the twentieth century.

> What is taking place here on Earth at the beginning of the twentieth century as the streaming of a number of personalities to the Anthroposophical Society had been prepared during the first half of the nineteenth century; souls had been brought together in the spiritual world, souls of these people who are incarnated today and who streamed in great numbers before they descended into the physical-sensory world. And a kind of cultus was conducted in the spiritual world at that time by a number of souls working together, a cultus that was a preparation for those longings that have arisen in the souls who, now incarnated, stream together to the Anthroposophical Society. *Anyone who has the gift of recognizing these souls in their bodies knows how they worked with him in the first half of the nineteenth century when mighty cosmic imaginations were placed into the supersensible world, imaginations that depict what I could call the new Christianity.* There [in the spiritual world] these souls were united—as they now are in bodies here on Earth—to assemble what I would call cosmic substantiality and cosmic forces into something that had real cosmic significance in its mighty pictures and

was the overture for what is to occur here on Earth as anthroposophical teaching and deeds. I might say: the vast majority of anthroposophists sitting here together could—if they were able to understand this fact—say to one another: Yes, we know one another; we were in the spiritual world together and had mighty cosmic imaginations together in a supersensible cultus![118]

According to Rudolf Steiner, the contents of this cosmic cultus were "mighty images of a future existence" that would have to be sought out by the members of the Michael community in a "changed form" during their subsequent earthly existence.[119]

Thus, beginning at the turning point in time, the cosmic formation of the Michael community took place in three central developmental steps. Two steps occurred in the sphere of the Sun (in the intervals between three different incarnations, along the path after death); the third and final, on the other hand, bordered the Earth, playing out in a last step before a next incarnation. Then the Michael community was to begin forming an earthly vessel in the twentieth century—and create that "Anthroposophical Society" that was intended to serve as an organ for a decisive future activity of the "Christ–Michael." These souls were to find one another within this Society, and it was their task to collaborate on "what was intended to assert itself in the Earth's development, and do so through Anthroposophy in the Michaelic sense."[120]

꩜

At the beginning of the twentieth century Rudolf Steiner actually began "gathering" these people with his anthroposophical lectures, people whose path of incarnation included Anthroposophy and the Anthroposophical Society.[121] He greeted the individuals who found their way there—sometimes with a surprising, humorous but serious statement: "I have been waiting here for you a long time."[122] And he did his best to see to it that the seeking souls could form a community with one another, or could find one another again in the depths of their being through this community.[123] Rudolf Steiner encouraged their meetings and conferences, and worked tirelessly for their awakening—in their "I" (*"Awaken in your 'I'"*),[124] in their social connection, and in the tasks they saw as given them by destiny or in a particular situation.

In and through his anthroposophical Spiritual Science, Rudolf Steiner set forth how the spiritualization of intelligence in the Michael sense could, in fact, be accomplished and put into practice in life. Through his lectures and writings he showed his pupils that understanding developed through ideas made it possible for them to begin recognizing how Michael wisdom and the activity of Michael impulses could be translated into concrete deeds in contemporary civilization.

Rudolf Steiner expected the developing spiritual community to be in a position to take the next steps during the coming years, based on the inner meaning of what they had heard, read, and experienced together. Confident in the self-knowledge to be found within the higher "I," Rudolf Steiner was already beginning to reveal details of the destiny relationships in the Anthroposophical Society at the end of 1910 (*Occult History*).[125] He even wrote the Mystery dramas for the members of his Society in order to support them in becoming aware of the spiritual challenges and tasks they had as individuals and as a community.

Rudolf Steiner also knew how helpful the Dornach building could be—as a tangible task for the community—in recalling cosmic Michael memories in the individual and the

Anthroposophical Society.[126] The architectural forms, the motifs of sculpture and painting, were connected with the Michael Mysteries and the content of the Michael School that had been given cosmic-cultic form only a short time earlier, a content experienced once again by the community through the imaginative depictions of that cultic form ("a mighty unfolding in pictures of spiritual life, the beings of the cosmos, the beings of the hierarchies"). Moreover, the establishment of an influential School for Spiritual Science, which Rudolf Steiner connected explicitly with the Dornach building project from the outset, was without doubt the *central* task of the Michael community in the twentieth century. With the spiritualization of thinking as the starting point, materialism in the individual fields of life and professional endeavors also had to be overcome—and it was no accident that Rudolf Steiner gave his first great Michael lectures during the same year that the foundation stone was laid in Dornach. These lectures indirectly provided a preliminary outline of the Dornach School's knowledge-based task and sought to prepare the members of the community for that task.[127]

The foundation stone laying on September 20, 1913, thereby acquired vital significance—and Rudolf Steiner once again hoped that what was being attempted on the Dornach hill and why destiny had led them there would become clear to those present (or at least to a *significant part* or *core* group of them). However, there was no breakthrough in consciousness—nor in karma consciousness—within the community. Nonetheless, over the short term—or even a bit longer—Rudolf Steiner continued to have confidence in it. During the years that followed, he repeatedly recalled the event and did so with clear intent; it was altogether foreign to him to promote a culture of "anniversaries" that had no tangible spiritual purpose.

In fact, however, during all the years that followed September 20, 1913, the people who felt that they were part of Anthroposophy encountered not only difficulties personally and with one another, but also the vast majority did not really understand what was at the heart of Rudolf Steiner's interest in the Anthroposophical Society and the Dornach School. Their lack of understanding had a debilitating effect on the actual impulse even though Rudolf Steiner himself continued to work tirelessly. "Thus what I actually want was constantly curtailed by the [Anthroposophical] Society. The force of the impulse was taken from it."[128] Conditions during World War I and the post-war period were determined by other forces—forces that intended just the opposite of the Michael stream; they made the advance of Anthroposophy within the life of society more difficult, while outer and inner constraints and missteps worked to complement and reinforce one another (the constellation of forces underlying them were often the same).

The situation grew ever more tense from year to year, and Rudolf Steiner's work became more and more an "escape forward" (Emil Bock). For all of civilization it was a "time of great decisions, that great crisis spoken of by all the holy books down through the ages."[129] ("Many decisions, enormous decisions are being made at the present time for humanity."[130]) Unlike many of his coworkers and followers, Rudolf Steiner knew that the spiritualization of the forces of intelligence in the Michael sense was a *pressing* necessity of the age if the threatened union between intelligence and the powers of evil—technological destruction and annihilation—were to be opposed in a timely way. "If we look out at the world today, there is and has been for years an extraordinary amount of destructive material available. Forces are at work that give us a sense of the abysses toward which western civilization is still heading."[131] In this situation, it was urgent for the anthroposophists who belonged to the Michael community by destiny to become active as "Michael's helpers" in the "mastery of the intelligence that fell from heaven to the Earth"—"more than any other battle, this battle is set in the human heart."[132]

With the Christmas Conference, the new founding of the Anthroposophical Society and the School for Spiritual Science at the end of 1923, Rudolf Steiner ventured his final attempt—just fifteen months before his death—to remind the anthroposophical community of its destiny tasks and the need to penetrate them with all the forces of consciousness available to them. ("All of the Society's karmic streams should find and unite with one another on a shared spiritual foundation within Anthroposophy as the modern Michaelic form of esoteric Christianity."—Prokofieff[133])

In his karma lectures, Rudolf Steiner shed light on the details of the cosmic background of the Michael community for the first time; furthermore, he opened an "Esoteric School of the Goetheanum" that was connected anew with the cosmic "Michael School" and had as its content "inner teachings of the heart" in mantric form.[134] In the course of the Christmas Conference, he also created a spiritual foundation stone for the Anthroposophical Society, a foundation stone woven of lofty spiritual forces; and he entrusted it to the heart, the destiny organ of the members.[135] Rudolf Steiner spoke directly and candidly about how the being of Anthroposophy and the Michael mission lay "sleeping" or "dreamily," "most deeply within the hearts" of the majority of anthroposophists, in the form of an "unconscious mystery."[136]

If they did not wish to neglect their world-historical task—a task that had been predetermined and prepared for centuries, indeed for more than two millennia—they had to begin in haste as a cohesive community to "take it to heart" and become genuinely active with an "inner holy diligence." To do otherwise had far-reaching consequences for the advancement of human civilization and for life on Earth. During the summer of 1924, Rudolf Steiner spoke for the first time about how this process of awakening—through taking up the Christmas Conference, through penetrating the spiritual foundation stone in one's heart, through a genuine understanding of the karma lectures, and by pursuing the esoteric path of the First Class [of the School for Spiritual Science]—would make possible a hastened reincarnation by leading anthroposophists at the end of the twentieth century. United with the incarnated Platonists from the medieval School of Chartres, they would together lead Anthroposophy and its civilizing capacity to an initial and urgently needed culmination.

The anthroposophical movement that began shortly after the turn of the nineteenth into the twentieth century had been carried essentially by the Aristotelian–Dominican wing of the Michael community; unlike events in the Middle Ages, it was necessary to allow the incarnation of the Aristotelian souls to precede the Platonic souls at this point—*because* the most important thing was to overcome scientific-materialistic thinking through the spiritualization of the intellect in the present time, and *because* this battle had to serve as the foundation for everything that would follow. ("It was necessary for those individuals who had been active more or less as Aristotelians to descend first; for under the influence of intellectualism the time had not yet come to deepen spirituality anew."[137]) Rudolf Steiner's philosophical anthroposophical writings, as well as countless numbers of his lecture courses, had prepared the way decisively in this Aristotelian way; even the founding of the Dornach School had its own place in this task and purpose from the very beginning. Rudolf Steiner wrote in a spring 1924 retrospective about what had been anticipated and begun during the last eleven years:

> When the construction of the building began Anthroposophy had already discovered members who were scientifically trained and working in the most diverse areas and who therefore found it possible to apply spiritual scientific methods to individual sciences; thus I was able to suggest adding the "School for Spiritual Science" to the name of the building.[138]

Rudolf Steiner reported in his karma lectures that the Platonists and the Aristotelians in the Michael community had—in the course of a "heavenly council" at the beginning of the thirteenth century—already agreed upon a *"shared"* endeavor to be undertaken at the end of the twentieth century, one hundred years after the dawn of the new Michael Age and at the end of the "Kali Yuga," the "age of darkness." After 1879, the Aristotelians were to bring all of their energies to this work in earthly civilization; on the other hand, the "Platonic sort of souls"—the leaders and pupils of Chartres—were to wait until the end of the twentieth century and only then join the Aristotelians who had already returned. The two groups would continue the anthroposophical movement together "with a much more spiritual force," and would be able to provide a decisive impulse for the further development of spiritual life on the Earth.¹³⁹ According to Rudolf Steiner, the future of the anthroposophical movement, as well as the whole of Earth civilization depended on the success of this initiative that had been prepared for millennia and agreed to in detail eight hundred years earlier:

> I have indicated how those people who stand with full fervor within the anthroposophical movement will return at the end of the century in order that others will then unite with them; that will ultimately be a determining factor in the rescue of the Earth, of Earth civilization, from decay. That is the mission, I would say, of the anthroposophical movement; on the one hand, it lies heavily on our hearts and on the other it moves our hearts, inspires us. This mission must be acknowledged.¹⁴⁰

~

Rudolf Steiner's "expectation" that the Dornach School would develop rapidly at the end of World War I was not realized; in the end it cannot be said that within the Anthroposophical Society there was a real understanding for and engagement with the Christmas Conference impulse.¹⁴¹ Rudolf Steiner made it unmistakably clear that the potential development at the end of the century depended on a real immersion in the esoteric impulse for the Christmas Conference—the re-founding of the Society and the School for Spiritual Science—in every respect, and on a real understanding for that impulse; according to him, everything depended on the necessary "conditions" being met—hence on "free will."¹⁴² Thus the overarching lack of understanding for and adherence to the new esoteric impulses signaled a far-reaching catastrophe generally as well as along Rudolf Steiner's personal path; this ultimately led to his illness and death. ("He seemed almost weighed down by the failure of his adherents."—Friedrich Rittelmeyer[143])

The Michael community's failure to awaken to its nature and its tasks had a decisively burdensome effect on Rudolf Steiner's path and the advancement of the Michael impulse. Surrounded by attacks from highly aggressive forces (those working against him and Christ–Michael), Rudolf Steiner was unprotected by any effective community; instead he bore the additional burden of irresponsible personal behavior among the members, behavior that he took on—as the "karma of the Anthroposophical Society"—in utter devotion and in a mood of sacrifice, until it led to his complete martyrdom.[144] Marie Steiner wrote later of the martyr's death suffered by Rudolf Steiner "for which we all certainly share guilt as individuals and as a Society."[145]

Rudolf Steiner died, and in the decade following his departure from the Earth the Dornach founding that had begun with such hope fell largely into disarray—in internal destruction that came of insufficient awakening and transformation, or soul weaknesses that allowed access to forces that worked against progress and were profoundly anti-Christian. Under these conditions it was obviously impossible to speak of an accelerated return at the end of the twentieth century by Rudolf Steiner's pupils who demonstrated Aristotelian leanings and had been awakened occultly. And the predicted incarnation of the Michael community's Platonically inclined souls during the course of the twentieth century was made effectively more difficult if not largely impossible.

As Rudolf Steiner already remarked in an early esoteric lesson in October 1907: "Michael needs legions of helpers who battle on the physical plane for what he has already won on the astral plane. That is the great task we have to fulfill."[146] The situation on the "physical plane" faced by the spirits of the School of Chartres who were preparing for their incarnation and were possibly still in the Moon sphere was threatening and offered few or no prospects. The confrontation between the Aristotelian "advance guard" and the prevailing materialism in nearly every field of civilization had—with the exception of Rudolf Steiner's central contribution—largely come to naught; lacking sufficient consciousness, the anthroposophical community demonstrated little common purpose (or was virtually destroyed), and the century unfolded with totalitarian governmental systems characterized by materialism and a regressive atmosphere that represented a virtual perversion of what the consciousness soul age demanded.

The powers of death took over the leadership in most areas of civilization and gradually drove the twentieth century into the abyss—doing so in concert with those forces of evil that worked within the human being, forces that actually achieved the liaison with the power of intelligence that Rudolf Steiner had repeatedly described. During the twentieth century, approximately 187 million human souls died a violent earthly death in a world of weapons and annihilation, a world armed to the hilt and engineered along highly intelligent lines. For the first time, a world existed that made possible "total war" and industrially driven "genocide," as well as perfected means of torture—and brought about the earthly extinction of a vast portion of nature's realms and beings.

Over the briefest of times, social structures experienced dramatic erosion; the exploitation and domination of the Earth organism through capital, profiteering, and the ruthlessness of "leading" groups acquired an ahrimanic form and character in a way never before even remotely possible in the whole history of the Earth and humanity.[147] Ecological systems as well as many human soul capacities have successively collapsed while a digitally controlled media world—and the interests and forces active in it—already exercised an increasingly firm grip on children and young people and drew them in their direction. ("...Ahriman is already making and will continue to make the strongest—the very strongest—efforts to appropriate the intelligence fallen to human beings, to possess human beings, so that he would possess the intelligence in human heads..."[148])

It was exceedingly difficult for the Platonically inclined souls of the Michael community to incarnate into such a reality. In view of these realities, it was more than questionable how the Michael battle could be carried out in the future with any real prospect for success. Rudolf Steiner had described the passage through the pre-birth Moon sphere as a stage of development in which incarnating individualities not only organize an etheric body from cosmic forces, but also gain a preview of their future biographical destinies—a preview that can be so dramatic that they may occasionally retreat from their decision to incarnate, or may go through their intended earthly path in a deformed way because of the "shock" suffered before birth.[149]

The experience of powerlessness to which the former teachers at Chartres were most likely exposed during the twentieth century can hardly be overestimated; after all, these were individualities who had lived and worked on Earth in a Platonically prepared Mystery site that had a Christian approach and an atmosphere of great artistic beauty. In addition, we should not underestimate their experience of Rudolf Steiner's dramatic martyrdom as the initiated leader of the whole stream, a martyrdom that took place during his lifetime *and* after his death as the result of the lack of understanding for Anthroposophy and the distortions to which it was subjected.

In the context of their biographies, how could the Platonic souls manage to endure this anticipated ineffectuality on Earth? How could they bear the current situation of a culturally impoverished, shallow, and often perverted civilization (including the attacks on Anthroposophy and Rudolf Steiner), as well as the misuse and estrangement of Anthroposophy by individuals and forces that claimed to be anthroposophical but had no connection to Rudolf Steiner and the Michael community? In the face of this situation, how could someone plunge into the destiny of the Earth? "Michael can fully use only courageous people—inwardly courageous people."[150]

Despite all the setbacks and serious impediments to the Anthroposophical Society, Rudolf Steiner had never given up during his lifetime; just a few days before his death, he had even taken more members into the "esoteric School at the Goetheanum," the "First Class" of the earthly Michael School.[151] "The ways and means must be found to continue what was intended by Anthroposophy from the very beginning," he once said in another context[152]—and throughout the entire course of his biography he had always been vigilant for what was still possible despite all the adversities and the constellations opposing him. Rudolf Steiner had also created a powerful spiritual element with the spiritual foundation stone of the Anthroposophical Society, one that could serve the souls who—despite the missteps—would enter onto this path in the future, mindful of what they would encounter but also with a knowledge of where spiritual support and spiritual help could be found. At the very least, powers for resurrection could be acquired through the spiritual foundation stone which "by its very nature is 'not of this world'" (Prokofieff).[153]

These powers were able to withstand the forces of evil and estrangement, as well as to work against them. A "resurrection from powerlessness" was possible through spiritual encounter and work with the foundation stone, a resurrection gained from the resulting certainty about destiny that—despite adverse conditions and a wide range of dangers—allows one to advocate "rock solid and steadfast"[154] for what had always been intended by Rudolf Steiner since the start of the twentieth century. "The karma that works in the will…"[155]

Sergei O. Prokofieff was born in Moscow at the beginning of the second half of the twentieth century. During the Soviet communist regime, he began to prepare an extensive overview of the works, spiritual initiatives, and institutions developed by Rudolf Steiner—the spiritual foundation stone, the esoteric of the First Class and of the Christmas Conference 1923/24, anthroposophical Christology and the founding of the School for Spiritual Science, the character of the anthroposophical karma-based community, the spiritual-scientific path of schooling, the basis for a collaboration in the future between Central and Eastern Europe (as the center of the next cultural epoch), but also the abysses of evil Rudolf Steiner described, as well as the course of Rudolf Steiner's life in the context of the New Mysteries.

The initiate leader of the New Mysteries, Rudolf Steiner, had hoped and had built on the hope that a time would come when the content of anthroposophical Spiritual Science would be researched in detail and could appear in all its spiritual fullness before a consciousness that *recognizes* it—in a "Platonically" formed overview of the whole of Anthroposophy, and in its inspired furtherance by those individualities who had actively taken part in the "Aristotelian" beginnings at the outset of the twentieth century. When Sergei O. Prokofieff began his thorough work, he did so aware of what until then had failed and what remained undone but was still needed for the future to counter effectively the situation of the times and the internal hindrances that had delayed the "culmination" of Anthroposophy foretold by Rudolf Steiner:

> We must still be tested to determine how prepared we are to stand in the world as true representatives of the esoteric impulse of the Christmas Conference, and to determine whether we ourselves are willing to engage in the realization of its aims and tasks regardless of all the failures and the setbacks of the Anthroposophical Society in the last [the twentieth] century.[156]

Sergei O. Prokofieff wrote about the need for individualities to step forward who "genuinely recognize the extraordinary difficulties of the tasks facing us and who will struggle to the end for their realization."[157] However, he also experienced the absence or the scarcity of great contemporaneous figures. The vital quality that had pulsed through Rudolf Steiner's character and work lived directly on in the first generations of anthroposophists who came immediately after him. A significant number of independent individualities were engaged in the continued progress of the work with both quantitative and qualitative success in applied cultural realms within the life of Anthroposophy: the schools, the homes where curative education is practiced, medical practices, and farms—but also within the whole of Anthroposophy itself.

By the last decades of the twentieth century—at the latest—it had nevertheless become unmistakably clear that the Anthroposophical Society as a whole had not only fallen far behind in its spiritual tasks and goals but was also losing sight of them more and more, including the memory of the laying of the building's foundation stone as well as the whole spiritual aspect of the founding of the School for Spiritual Science and its connection to the age of Michael. The Society emphatically distanced itself from the being of Rudolf Steiner—a development that had begun during his lifetime in a way that made his biography difficult and in the end more burdensome, ultimately contributing to his grievous suffering and early death.

Leading individualities of the Michael community who were to incarnate during the twentieth century knew about these conditions. They themselves were faced with similar and additional difficulties insofar as they actually started to follow Rudolf Steiner and take part in building the Anthroposophical Society as an effective Michael community on Earth despite the massive counter forces. "Do I myself want to follow Rudolf Steiner on his path of sacrifice, regardless of the difficulties and sufferings connected with it—or do I not?" (Prokofieff).[158] In all likelihood, this question arose not only from an earthly perspective, but also among leading individualities of the Michael community during the time immediately before birth, and this led to delays and circuitous paths.

What was asked for was the will "to travel the path of responsibilities and service and thereby to allow oneself to be guided by the example of Rudolf Steiner,"[159] and further to have the courage to withstand the "trial of powerlessness" and—despite all the other warnings, symptoms, and occurrences—to continue to trust in a breakthrough into civilization by the Michael stream. In Arnheim during the summer of 1924, Rudolf Steiner foretold that during the twentieth century humanity would find itself "at the grave of all civilization," or at the beginning of that age "when the Michael battle for the Michael impulse will be fought in human souls who connect intelligence and spirituality in their hearts."[160] In view of the far-reaching processes of destruction with an ahrimanic provenance and intelligence, processes that consumed territory after territory, and in view of the many twentieth-century developments associated with them, it was more than apparent which of the two alternative directions had prevailed in the "time of great decisions," at least from a global perspective.

Michaelic prospects for further work did arise, however, in the context of the actual Christmas Conference and an understanding of its profoundest content.[161] It was not at all the case that Rudolf Steiner's own initiatives and his statement of the esoteric goal—in the sense of the Michael stream and the Christmas Conference—had been lost on all of his coworkers. Even though the Anthroposophical Society as such had been unable to achieve a new level, and despite the fact that difficulties were already evident in 1924/25, what Rudolf Steiner's closest coworkers and many friends had experienced with him affected them profoundly and reached deep into their souls. An awakening to destiny had begun already in their lifetime on various levels, and Rudolf Steiner's presentations about the path of the Michael community and its karma had shaken many in his audience to the core.

> I am preparing myself for this new era from the twentieth into the twenty-first century—says a genuine anthroposophical soul to itself—because there are many

destructive forces on the Earth. All of cultural life, the whole life of civilization on the Earth must fall into decadence if the spirituality of the Michael impulse is not taken hold of by humanity, if human beings are not in a position to lift up again the part of civilization that wills to go downhill today. If such genuine anthroposophical souls are found, souls who want to carry spirituality in this way into the life of the Earth, a movement upward will occur. If such souls are not found then the decadence will continue to roll on. The World War with all of its evil side effects will be only the beginning of an even greater evil. Humanity today faces a far-reaching eventuality: the eventuality of either watching everything about civilization slide into the abyss or lifting it up instead through spirituality, moving it forward in the sense of what is set forth in the Michael impulse, an impulse that stands with the Christ impulse.[162]

Rudolf Steiner spoke to hundreds, even thousands of people who were members of the Anthroposophical Society—as well as to those individuals he thought of as such. ("If such genuine anthroposophical souls are found...") For people like Ita Wegman it was clear that all was not lost—despite the devastation of the Anthroposophical Society (that she knew very well and that she herself had endured), and despite Central Europe's collapse into war during the 1930s and '40s.

At the beginning of the thirteenth century, the leading spirits of the School of Chartres had come quickly to an agreement with the Aristotelians who were approaching their next incarnation during which they were to create the Dominican community. The agreement concerned the further course of action for the emerging century but also far into the future (including the dawning of the new Michael Age and beyond). Ita Wegman shared with a small circle of friends that in the spiritual world Rudolf Steiner would also gather together souls connected to him and to Christ–Michael, and with their leading individualities consider the further course of action—in light of developments during the twentieth century. As farsighted and sensibly organized as this course of action for the beginning and end of the twentieth century had been—and as dramatic and consequential as its failure was (at least in part)—it was just as clear for Ita Wegman that Rudolf Steiner and the leading spirits of the Michael stream would never give up under any circumstances.

Until her death on March 4, 1943, Ita Wegman was engaged and active to assure that the esoteric and social impulse of Anthroposophy's work *around the world* would not vanish, and that Rudolf Steiner's lectures and writings were available in many world languages. She aimed toward the future and was herself prepared to traverse the path of suffering in the twentieth century to its end—just as Rudolf Steiner had done. As Sergei O. Prokofieff wrote more than a half-century after Ita Wegman's death:

> It is Anthroposophy that reveals for us the knowledge of the spiritual aims of the living Christ, and the Christmas Conference leads us to an understanding of Rudolf Steiner's own goals. That carries in it the possibility of following Rudolf Steiner along his inner path, a path that is, in fact, nothing other than the contemporary path of the "imitation of Christ."[163]

He cited the farewell contained in the fifteenth chapter of the Gospel of John, from the Russian Gospel: "No one has a greater love than this, that he lay down his soul for his friends" (John 15:13).

Just a few weeks before her death, Madeleine van Deventer, Ita Wegman's representative and successor in Arlesheim, enthusiastically welcomed Sergei O. Prokofieff's first fundamental work published in German (1982); it concerned Rudolf Steiner and the basis for the New Mysteries.[164] In it there was something new that led to the future and might still be capable of realizing the great spiritual awakening of the Anthroposophical Society that Rudolf Steiner had described as possible after the end of the twentieth century. Ita Wegman and Madeleine van Deventer experienced Sergei O. Prokofieff's activity at the Goetheanum as it radiated into the Anthroposophical Society worldwide (after Easter 2001)—however, they no longer did so from an earthly perspective.

Based on the evidence offered by their lives and knowing their spiritual personalities (and individualities), it is nevertheless possible to surmise that they—together with Marie Steiner and Elizabeth Vreede—greeted this deed wholeheartedly. It was clear to all of them that the world needs a powerfully active, spiritually impressive Goetheanum, a Goetheanum in a position to represent the esotericism of Anthroposophy, the Anthroposophical Society, and the School for Spiritual Science at a high level. Furthermore, they knew from personal experience what it means to shoulder the "cross of the Anthroposophical Society" and to bear it—in harmony with Rudolf Steiner's being:

> As a result we will gradually approach the sphere of the spiritual world where Rudolf Steiner continues today to bear the karma of the Anthroposophical Society. In order to find him there, however, we must decide to share this karma with him and to shoulder at least a small portion of his cross with our still-weak forces.[165]

In 1925, Ita Wegman had termed the Christmas Conference and Rudolf Steiner's connection to the Anthroposophical Society a "*Christ deed.*" ("Just as the Christ-being connected Himself with the Earth for the wellbeing of humanity, Rudolf Steiner identified himself with the Anthroposophical Society. It was a Christ deed."[166]) Rudolf Steiner had taken the karma of the Anthroposophical Society onto himself. And living within the Michael stream in emulation of him requires a readiness that was to be developed through him and through the Mystery of Golgotha, a readiness to take the paths and the missteps of others into one's own destiny and to carry them forward as such. "*Anthroposophy was given to us to broaden and spiritualize our consciousness, to strengthen our sense of responsibility, and to awaken our will to fulfill our tasks.*"[167]

In view of the actual historical situation of the Anthroposophical Society and movement in the twentieth century, the appearance and singular activity of the Michaelite Sergei O. Prokofieff has extraordinary meaning. This remains true even if his work since 1983 (its spiritual content and purpose) has been insufficiently recognized and sometimes tragically underappreciated, including by those within various leadership bodies of the Anthroposophical Society. Ita Wegman often told her coworkers in regard to Rudolf Steiner: "Your perception of him is always much too small." Her words are valid in this situation as well.

Sergei O. Prokofieff's extraordinary "courage to bear witness" and his fidelity to the esoteric core of the Anthroposophical Society in times of crisis and danger serve to demonstrate "what the Michael power, the Michael-being actually *wants* from the human being."[168] His path offers testimony to the fact that—despite all the hindrances—it was still possible and meaningful for the leading spirits of the Michael community to incarnate and work in service to Anthroposophy during the dramatic twentieth century that had nearly gone lost, three decades after Rudolf Steiner's death—that is, to follow, undeterred, the predetermined path of destiny within the contemporary anthroposophical community, and to withstand all the tests and trials of powerlessness and doubt. ("But to those souls who are anthroposophical souls it is said: You will continue to be tested in your courage to bear witness to what you can perceive clearly as a voice because of the inclination of your soul life, because of the inclination of your heart."[169])

In *May Human Beings Hear It!* (2004), Sergei O. Prokofieff explained that a part of this trial or test is the willingness to become a martyr, "without which we are unable to pursue the path of Christ discipleship today."[170] What it really means to gain inspirations and impulses to act from the source of the New Mysteries—to fulfill the event of the Christmas Conference anew in one's own life—is tangible in him, in Sergei O. Prokofieff, in his spiritually illuminated work and "creative spirituality."[171] Thus for *all* those who feel deeply and inwardly dedicated to Rudolf Steiner, Anthroposophy, and the Anthroposophical Society, he can serve as a shining model, a far-reaching radiance, a helper in the spirit, and a powerfully active preparer of the future.

> Insofar as the members of the Society work toward their spiritual aims...out of a genuine—i.e., truly esoteric—understanding of the Christmas Conference, the success of this work can even today bring together the movement and the Society, or (each time) bring them together anew—if only the members really want this and are prepared to *act out of knowledge*.[172]

Sei in Zeit und Ewigkeit
Schüler im Lichte Michaels
In der Götter Liebe
In des Kosmos Höhen.

Be in time and eternity
A pupil in the light of Michael
In the love of the gods
In the heights of the cosmos.[173]

Notes

1. Sergei O. Prokofieff, *Die Esoterik der Anthroposophischen Gesellschaft* [The esoteric nature of the Anthroposophical Society] (Dornach, 2012), p. 16; English edition forthcoming.
2. *Mantrische Sprüche. Seelenübungen II* [Mantric verses. Soul exercises II] (Collected Works [CW] 268), p. 349.
3. Rudolf Steiner, "Kunst- und Lebensfragen im Lichte der Geisteswissenschaft" [Questions of art and life in the light of Spiritual Science] (CW 162), p. 47; lecture, May 24, 1915.
4. CW 268, p. 345.
5. Ibid., p. 346 (emphasis by the author).
6. Ibid., p. 345.
7. Rudolf Steiner, "Schicksalszeichen auf dem Entwickelungswege der Anthroposophischen Gesellschaft" [Signs of destiny on the developmental path of the Anthroposophical Society] (Dornach, 1943), p. 36; lecture, Sept. 19, 1914.
8. Ibid., "Zum inneren Zusammenhang der Stuttgarter Waldorfschulgründung (vom Herbst 1919) mit dieser Inkarnationssituation kommender Menschenseelen" [The inner connection between the founding of the Stuttgart Waldorf School (autumn 1919) and this incarnation situation for future human souls]. See also Peter Selg, *Rudolf Steiner, 1861–1925. Lebens- und Werkgeschichte* [Rudolf Steiner, 1861–1925: His life and work], vol. 2 (Arlesheim, 2012), pp. 1,471 ff.
9. CW 268, op cit, p. 345.
10. Ibid., p. 347.
11. See Rudolf Steiner, *The Fifth Gospel: From the Akashic Record*, London: Rudolf Steiner Press, 1967 (CW 148); and Peter Selg, *Rudolf Steiner and the Fifth Gospel: Insights Into a New Understanding of the Christ Mystery*, Great Barrington, MA: SteinerBooks, 2009.
12. Ibid., pp. 66ff.
13. See Peter Selg, *Rudolf Steiner, 1861–1925*, op cit, pp. 569ff.
14. See also Rudolf Steiner, *Die menschliche Seele in ihrem Zusammenhang mit göttlich-geistigen Individualitäten* [The human soul in its connection with divine-spiritual individualities] (CW 224),

pp. 148ff (lecture, May 7, 1923); and Sergei O. Prokofieff, "Easter, Ascension, and Whitsun in the Light of Anthroposophy," in *The Mystery of the Resurrection in the Light of Anthroposophy*, London: Temple Lodge, 2010, pp. 47ff.

15. Rudolf Steiner, *Das Geheimnis des Todes. Wesen und Bedeutung Mitteleuropas und die europäischen Volksgeister* [The secret of death: The nature and meaning of Central Europe and the spirit of the European people] (CW 159), p. 289, lecture, May 18, 1915 (in English: *Christ in Relation to Lucifer and Ahriman*, New York: Anthroposophic Press, 1978).

16. Cited in Peter Selg, *Christian Morgenstern. Sein Weg mit Rudolf Steiner* [Christian Morgenstern: His path with Rudolf Steiner] (Stuttgart, 2008), pp. 260f.

17. Rudolf Steiner, *Anthroposophische Leitsätze. Der Erkenntnisweg der Anthroposophie—Das Michael-Mysterium* [in English: *Anthroposophical Leading Thoughts. Anthroposophy as a Path of Knowledge: The Michael Mystery*, London: Rudolf Steiner Press, 1999] (CW 26), p. 14.

18. Rudolf Steiner, *Die spirituellen Hintergründe der äußeren Welt. Der Sturz der Geister der Finsternis* [in English: *The Fall of the Spirits of Darkness*, London: Rudolf Steiner Press, 2008] lecture, Oct. 7, 1917 (CW 177), p. 97;

19. Rudolf Steiner, *Schicksalsbildung und Leben nach dem Tode* [in English: *Spiritual Life Now and after Death: Forming Our Destiny in the Physical and Spiritual Worlds*, Great Barrington, MA: SteinerBooks, 2012] (CW 157a), p. 71; lecture, Nov. 20, 1915.

20. See eg., Steiner, *Vom Menschenrätsel. Ausgesprochenes und Unausgesprochenes im Denken, Schauen, Sinnen einer Reihe deutscher und österreichischer Persönlichkeiten* [in English: *The Riddle of Man: From the Thinking, Observations and Contemplations of a Series of German and Austrian Personalities*, Spring Valley, NY: Mercury Press, 1990] (CW 20).

21. Rudolf Steiner, *Soziale Ideen–Soziale Wirklichkeit–Soziale Praxis* [Social ideas, social realities, social praxis], vol. 1 (CW 337a), p. 324.

22. Rudolf Steiner, *Die Weltgeschichte in anthroposophischer Beleuchtung* [in English: *World History and the Mysteries in the Light of Anthroposophy*, London: Rudolf Steiner Press, 1997] (CW 233), p. 113; lecture, Dec. 29, 1923.

23. Rudolf Steiner, *Anthroposophische Gemeinschaftsbildung* [in English: *Awakening to Community*, London: Rudolf Steiner Press, 1974] (CW 257), p. 20 (emphasis by the author); lecture, Jan. 23, 1923.

24. Rudolf Steiner, *Die Weihnachtstagung zur Begründung der Allgemeinen Anthroposophischen Gesellschaft 1923/24* [in English: *The Christmas Conference: For the Foundation of the General Anthroposophical Society, 1923/1924*, Hudson, NY: Anthroposophic Press, 1990] (CW 260), p. 50 (Bylaws).
25. CW 233, p. 154 [in English: *World History and the Mysteries*, op cit]; lecture, Jan. 1, 1924.
26. Rudolf Steiner, *Anthroposophie, ihre Erkenntniswurzeln und Lebenfrüchte* [in English: *Fruits of Anthroposophy*, London: Rudolf Steiner Press, 1986] (CW 78), p. 150; lecture, Sept. 9, 1921.
27. CW 268, op cit, p. 351.
28. Ibid., p. 350.
29. Rudolf Steiner, "Wege zu einem neuen Baustil. 'Und der Bau wird Mensch'" [in English: *Architecture as a Synthesis of the Arts*, London: Rudolf Steiner Press, 1999] (CW 286), p. 29; lecture, Dec. 12, 1911.
30. "About 70 meters away from us...Rudolf Steiner moved in an arc—forward, sideways, and backward again—often raising his eyes to the stars; he sometimes held his walking stick out toward the stars as well. Then Rudolf Steiner began feeling around in a small area with his stick, almost constantly looking up to the stars; he stopped short, and suddenly he thrust his stick into the earth and called 'This is the spot.'" (Wilhelm Schrack, "Eine Erinnerung aus der Zeit vor der Grundsteinlegung 1913" [A memory from the time before the foundation stone laying in 1913], in *Mitteilungen aus der anthroposophischen Arbeit in Deutschland* Christmas 1953). Reprinted in Erika von Baravalle (ed.), *Rudolf Steiners Grundsteinlegung vom 20. Sept. 1913* (forthcoming).
31. Cited in Erika von Baravalle, "Zur Komposition des Grundsteins" [On the composition of the foundation stone] in Erika von Baravalle (ed.), *Rudolf Steiners Grundsteinlegung.*
32. Max Benzinger, "Ein Augenzeuge der Grundsteinlegung berichtet" [An eyewitness report on the foundation stone laying], in Erika Beltle and Kurt Vierl (eds.), *Erinnerungen an Rudolf Steiner* [Memories of Rudolf Steiner] (Stuttgart, 1979), p. 151.
33. Ibid., p. 150.
34. "What happened here was what always happened (even if it shouldn't)—immediately [after Rudolf Steiner announced the time] the telephones were activated and other members were informed, although only the members who were there were involved" (ibid.).
35. Cited in Erika von Baravalle, "Es werde verhüllt! Zum Vorgang und Wortlaut des Grundsteinlegungsaktes für das Erste Goetheanum"

[Let it be ensheathed! On the process and words for the foundation stone laying of the First Goetheanum], in *Das Goetheanum. Nachrichtenblatt für Mitglieder,* 38:2004; reprinted in Erika von Baravalle, ed., *Rudolf Steiners Grundsteinlegung.*
36. Ibid.
37. See Erika von Baravalle, "Vom Mysterium der Grundsteinlegung" [On the Mystery of the foundation stone laying] in *Das Goetheanum. Nachrichtenblatt für Mitglieder* 38:2003; reprinted in *Rudolf Steiners Grundsteinlegung vom 20. Sept. 1913.*
38. CW 268, op cit, p. 241.
39. See Peter Selg, *Rudolf Steiner and Christian Rosenkreutz,* Great Barrington, MA: SteinerBooks, 2012, pp. 48ff.
40. See Ernst Bindel, "Die sinnbildliche Bedeutung des Pentagon-Dodekaeders als Grundstein geistig bedeutsamer Bauten" [The emblematic meaning of the pentagon-dodecahedron as the foundation stone for spiritually significant buildings], and Erika von Baravalle, "Zur Komposition des Grundsteins" [On the composition of the foundation stone], in Erika von Baravalle (ed.), *Rudolf Steiners Grundsteinlegung.*
41. Cited in Erika von Baravalle, "Es werde verhüllt! Zum Vorgang und Wortlaut des Grundsteinlegungsaktes für das Erste Goetheanums."
42. See Rudolf Steiner, *Das Initiaten-Bewusstsein. Die wahren und die falschen Wege der geistigen Forschung* [in English: *True and False Paths in Spiritual Investigation,* London: Rudolf Steiner Press, 1985] (CW 243), pp. 54f; lecture, Aug. 13,1924; see also Erika von Baravalle, "Zur Komposition des Grundsteins."
43. See Rudolf Steiner, *Anthroposophical Leading Thoughts* (CW 26), op cit, pp. 167ff (essay of Jan. 25, 1925), on the contemporary and thematic context of this work; see also Peter Selg, *Rudolf Steiner, 1861–1925,* vol. 3, pp. 2,090ff
44. See Rudolf Steiner, *Anthroposophical Leading Thoughts* (CW 26), op cit, "The Activity of Michael and the Future of Mankind," pp. 81ff.
45. Ibid., p. 200.
46. See Rudolf Steiner, *Die Brücke zwischen der Weltgeistigkeit und dem Physischen des Menschen. Die Suche nach der neuen Isis, der göttlichen Sophia* [in English: *The Bridge between Universal Spirituality and the Physical Constitution of Man,* Great Barrington, MA: SteinerBooks, 2007] (CW 202), pp. 187ff (lecture, Dec. 18, 1920); and Peter Selg, *"Die beseelte Menschen-Sonne." Eine Herz-Meditation Rudolf Steiners* ["The ensouled human-sun." A heart meditation by Rudolf Steiner] (Arlesheim, 2011), pp. 23ff.

47. CW 268, op cit, p. 344.
48. Ibid.
49. Ibid., p. 345.
50. See Sergei O. Prokofieff, *Das Rätsel des menschlichen Ich. Eine anthroposophische Betrachtung* (Dornach, 2013), pp. 10ff; selections from this publication are contained in the addenda to Sergei O. Prokofieff, *Anthroposophy and the Philosophy of Freedom*, London: Temple Lodge, 2009.
51. CW 268, op cit, p. 346.
52. See Fritz Götte, "Der Menschenseele Sehnsuchtsschrei nach dem Geiste" [The human cry of yearning for the spirit], in *Mitteilungen aus der anthroposophischen Arbeit in Deutschland*. Michaelmas, 1973. Reprinted in Erika von Baravalle (ed.), *Rudolf Steiners Grundsteinlegung*.
53. See Sergei O. Prokofieff, *The Mystery of the Resurrection in the Light of Anthroposophy*, London: Temple Lodge, 2010, pp. 24ff; see also "The Mystery of the Resurrection in the Light of The Fifth Gospel," pp. 173ff, in Sergei O. Prokofieff and Peter Selg, *The Creative Power of Anthroposophical Christology*, Great Barrington, MA: SteinerBooks, 2012, as well as "The Nature of the First Goetheanum and the Mystery of Golgotha," pp. 113ff, in the same book.
54. "Mit einer Taufe muss ich getauft werden, und wie ist mir bang (wie werde ich zusammengepresst), bis sie vollendet ist." ["I must be baptized with a baptism, and how apprehensive I am (how constrained I feel) until it is fulfilled."] (Luke 12:50) Translation into German by Rudolf Frieling. On the relationship between the Baptism and Golgotha from the perspective of spiritual science, see Peter Selg, *Das Ereignis der Jordantaufe. Epiphanias im Urchristentum und in der Anthroposophie Rudolf Steiners* [The event of the baptism in the Jordan: Epiphany in primal Christianity and in Rudolf Steiner's Anthroposophy] (Stuttgart, 2008), pp. 63ff.
55. CW 268, op cit, p. 348.
56. See also the end of chapter 1 in Peter Selg, *The Lord's Prayer and Rudolf Steiner: A Study of His Insights into the Archetypal Prayer of Christianity*, Edinburgh: Floris Books, 2014.
57. See Peter Selg, *Rudolf Steiner and the School for Spiritual Science. The Foundation of the "First Class,"* Great Barrington, MA: SteinerBooks, 2012, pp. 15ff.
58. See Peter Selg, *Rudolf Steiner and Christian Rosenkreutz*, Great Barrington, MA: SteinerBooks, 2012, pp. 71ff.

59. See Andreas Neider's study, *Michael und die Apokalypse des 20. Jahrhunderts. Das Jahr 1913 im Lebensgang Rudolf Steiners* [Michael and the apocalypse of the 20th century. The year 1913 in the life of Rudolf Steiner] (Stuttgart, 2013).
60. In Rudolf Steiner, *Schicksalszeichen auf dem Entwickelüngswege der Anthroposophischen Gesellschaft*, op cit, p. 36; on Rudolf Steiner's Sept. 19, 1914, address, see Peter Selg, *Die Gestalt Christi. Rudolf Steiner und die geistige Intention des zentralen Goetheanum-Kunstwerkes* (Arlesheim, 2009), pp. 18ff [in English: *The Figure of Christ: Rudolf Steiner and the Spiritual Intention behind the Goetheanum's Central Work of Art*, London: Temple Lodge, 2009, pp. 9ff].
61. Christian Morgenstern, *Werke und Briefe. Bd. 2. Lyrik 1906–1914* [Works and letters, vol. 2: Lyrics, 1906–1914] (ed.), Martin Kießig (Stuttgart, 1992), p. 205.
62. CW 268, op cit, p. 344.
63. Ibid.
64. In Erika von Baravalle (ed.), *Rudolf Steiners Grundsteinlegung vom 20 Sept. 1913.*
65. CW 233, op cit, p. 147 (emphasis by the author).
66. Rudolf Steiner, *Zur Geschichte und aus den Inhalten der ersten Abteilung der Esoterischen Schule von 1904 bis 1914* [in English: *From the History and Contents of the First Section of the Esoteric School: Letters, Documents, and Lectures: 1904–1914*, Great Barrington, MA: SteinerBooks, 2010] (CW 264), p. 431; lecture, Dec. 15, 1911.
67. CW 268, op cit, p. 344.
68. Cited in Erika von Baravalle, "Es werde verhüllt! Zum Vorgang und Wortlaut des Grundsteinlegungsaktes für das Erste Goetheanums."
69. Rudolf Steiner, *Individuelle Geistwesen and ihr Wirken in der Seele des Menschen* [in English: *Secret Brotherhoods and the Mystery of the Human Double*, London: Rudolf Steiner Press, 2011] (CW 178), p. 175; lecture, Nov. 18, 1917.
70. Rudolf Steiner, *Das esoterische Christentum und die geistige Führung der Menschheit* [in English: *Esoteric Christianity and the Mission of Christian Rosenkreutz*, London: Rudolf Steiner Press, 2005] (CW 130), p. 235; lecture, Jan. 27, 1912.
71. CW 286, op cit, p. 25; lecture, Dec. 12, 1911.
72. See Peter Selg, *The Figure of Christ: Rudolf Steiner and the Spiritual Intention behind the Goetheanum's Central Work of Art*, London: Temple Lodge, 2009; and Sergei O. Prokofieff, *Rudolf*

Steiner's Sculptural Group: A Revelation of the Spiritual Purpose of Humanity and the Earth, London: Temple Lodge, 2013.
73. CW 268, op cit, p. 346.
74. CW 162, op cit, pp. 46ff; lecture, May 24, 1915.
75. Marie Steiner (ed.), *Die Sehnsucht der Seelen nach Geist. Ein Zeichen der Zeit. Worte Rudolf Steiners am ersten Jahrestag der Grundsteinlegung des Goetheanum in Dornach am 20. September 1914* [The yearning of souls for the spirit. A sign of the times. Rudolf Steiner's words at the first anniversary of the foundation stone laying for the Goetheanum on September 20, 1914] (Dornach, 1938), p. 20.
76. See Rudolf Steiner, *Menschliches Seelenleben und Geistesstreben im Zusammenhange mit Welt- und Erdenentwicklung* [in English: *The Human Soul in Relation to World Evolution,* New York: Anthroposophic Press, 1985] (CW 212), pp. 122ff (lecture of May 26, 1922); and Peter Selg, *The Mystery of the Heart: The Sacramental Physiology of the Heart in Aristotle, Thomas Aquinas, and Rudolf Steiner,* Great Barrington, MA: SteinerBooks, 2012, pp. 96ff.
77. Rudolf Steiner, *Esoterische Betrachtungen karmischer Zusammenhänge,* vol. 4 [in English: *Karmic Relationships: Esoteric Studies,* vol. 4, London: Rudolf Steiner Press, 2008] (CW 238), p. 73; lecture, Sept. 12, 1924.
78. "That, my dear friends, should be the quality that has entered the anthroposophical movement since the Christmas conference: that supersensible facts are dealt with in a completely open, natural way and in full consciousness of that knowledge. That should be the esoteric quality that runs through the anthroposophical movement. Only then will it be possible to give the anthroposophical movement its true spiritual content" (ibid., p. 72).
79. Ibid., p. 73.
80. Ibid., p. 72.
81. Rudolf Steiner, *Esoterische Betrachtungen karmischer Zusammenhänge,* vol. 3 [in English: *Karmic Relationships: Esoteric Studies,* vol. 3, London: Rudolf Steiner Press, 2002] (CW 237), p. 111; lecture, July 28, 1924.
82. See Rudolf Steiner's research results in this regard; in Peter Selg, *Das Kind als Sinnes-Organ. Zur Anthropologie der Nachahmungsvorgänge* [The child as sensory organ. The anthropology of imitative processes] (Arlesheim, forthcoming).
83. Rudolf Steiner, *Esoterische Betrachtungen karmischer Zusannnenhänge,* vol. 6 [in English: *Karmic Relationships: Esoteric Studies,*

vol. 6 London: Rudolf Steiner Press, 2002], vol. 6 (CW 240), p. 168; lecture, July 19, 1924.

84. In his Torquay lecture on August 21, 1924, Rudolf Steiner emphasized that Michael and his host saw the Christ "leaving the Sun at the time of the Mystery of Golgotha" (ibid., p. 239). Rudolf Steiner made clear in his lectures on the "Fifth Gospel" that the complete, or full, incarnation of the Christ-(Sun)-Spirit in the body of Jesus of Nazareth did not occur until Golgotha; thus it is quite likely that the spiritual "departure" from the Sun was also completed at that time.

85. See Sergei O. Prokofieff, *Und die Erde wird zur Sonne. Zum Mysterium der Auferstehung* [And the Earth will become a sun: On the Mystery of the Resurrection] (Arlesheim, 2012); English edition forthcoming.

86. Christian Morgenstern, *Werke und Briefe*, op cit, p. 222.

87. "For as long as the Earth has existed, Michael has been the regent of cosmic intelligence" (CW 240, op cit, p. 238; lecture, Aug. 21, 1924).

88. Ibid., p. 167; lecture, July 19, 1924.

89. On Aristotle's relation to the Mysteries of Eleusis and Ephesus, the "chthonic" Mysteries and those of the Cabiri ("Those who are being initiated into the Mysteries should not learn something; they should experience it and permit themselves to be put into a mood that makes them receptive—assuming that they are at all capable of such a thing" [Aristotle, *Fragmentum*, 15; cited in J.-M. Zemb, *Aristoteles*, Hamburg, 2002, p. 147]). See Rudolf Steiner's lectures of Dec. 15, 1926, and Dec. 27, 1923 (GA 233, op. cit.) [in English: *Mystery Knowledge and Mystery Centres,* London: Rudolf Steiner Press, 2013 (CW 232), and *World History and the Mysteries in the Light of Anthroposophy* (CW 233), op. cit.], as well as the lecture of Apr. 22, 1924 (*Mysterienstätten des Mittelalters*) (CW 233a). In his Dornach lecture of Dec. 29, 1923, Rudolf Steiner spoke of the history of consciousness and the step from Plato to Aristotle in the sense of a progressive "incarnation" of the power of thought: "Simply try to discover the difference between reading Plato and reading Aristotle through inner spiritual experience based on meditation. When modern individuals bring a background of genuine, true spiritual experience and a certain meditative foundation to reading Plato, after a while they will feel as if their heads were a bit above the physical head, as if they had expanded a little beyond the physical organism. This is absolutely the case for those who do not merely read Plato superficially. Things are different when reading Aristotle. With Aristotle you never have the feeling that the reading

takes you out of your body. But when those with a certain meditative preparation read Aristotle they will have the feeling that they are working right within the physical human being. The physical human being comes to the fore through Aristotle. It works. It is not logic that one simply apprehends, but logic that works inwardly" (CW 233, op. cit., pp. 103f [in English: *World History and the Mysteries,* op. cit.]).

90. Christian Morgenstern, *Werke und Briefe,* op cit, p. 223.
91. "At the Dawn of the Michael Age," in *Anthroposophical Leading Thoughts* (CW 26), op cit, p. 51.
92. CW 240, op cit, p. 169; lecture, July 19, 1924.
93. Ibid., pp. 150f; lecture, July 18, 1924.
94. Thomas Aquinas, *De unitate intellectus contra Averroistas;* German translation by Wolf-Ulrich Klünker (Stuttgart, 1987), p. 90.
95. CW 238, op cit, p. 66; lecture, Sept. 12, 1924.
96. CW 237, op cit, p. 111; lecture, July 28, 1924.
97. "[Michael] is seeking a new metamorphosis of his cosmic task. Earlier he allowed thoughts to stream into human souls from the outer spiritual world; since the last third of the nineteenth century he has wanted to live in human souls where the thoughts are being formed.... Now, in the Michael age, this [human] spirituality must no longer be experienced unconsciously; it must be experienced consciously in its uniqueness. That signifies the entry of the Michael being into the human soul" (CW 26, pp. 61, 66). Elsewhere Rudolf Steiner has said "that in the future intellectuality will stream through human hearts, but as the same power it was at the beginning when it streamed from divine-spiritual powers" (ibid., p. 114).
98. In Dornach on Sept. 12, 1924, Rudolf Steiner said the following (among other things) about the spiritual life of the School of Chartres: "One looks at this activity, sees how the teachers from Chartres wander on the earth, pursue their studies filled with visions, and how the inspiring ray from the Aristotelian soul in the realm above the Earth shines down into this and puts the Platonic element on the right path We then have an entirely different view of life than the one commonly held—in outer life we like to differentiate between Platonists and Aristotelians as though they were opposites. In fact, that is not at all the case. The epochs of the Earth require speaking in the Platonic sense at times, and at times in the Aristotelian sense. But if we look at the supersensible life behind sensory life, one fructifies the other, one is part of the other" (CW 238, pp. 66f).
99. CW 237, op cit, p. 101; lecture, July 13, 1924.

100. See Rudolf Steiner's corresponding research results in Peter Selg, *Unbornness: Human Pre-existence and the Journey toward Birth,* Great Barrington, MA: SteinerBooks, 2010, pp. 29ff.
101. Ibid., pp. 29–30.
102. CW 240, op cit, p. 191; lecture, July 20, 1924.
103. Ibid., p. 248; lecture, Aug. 21, 1924. There Rudolf Steiner offers the following further explanation: "But a great and mighty supersensible institution for wisdom was founded under the leadership of Michael himself; all those souls were gathered who had been touched by heathenism but still sought Christianity, and also those souls who had once lived on the Earth during the first Christian centuries with Christianity (as it was at that time) in their hearts. A Michael host formed, one that lived in supersensible regions and received there the teachings of the Michael teachers from the ancient time of Alexander, the Michael teachers from the time of the Grail tradition, and the Michael teachers who had been present in impulses like the Arthurian impulse. Every possible soul with a Christian nuance felt itself drawn to this Michael community..." (ibid., pp. 248f).
104. CW 237, op cit, p. 112; lecture, July 28, 1924.
105. Ibid., p. 113.
106. "It was something that was—so to speak—an exception to all the other activities that regularly took place between gods and human beings. The souls connected with Michael—the leading human souls from the time of Alexander, those from the great age of the Dominicans, those who had been their followers, and a large number of striving, developing human beings connected with the leading spirits—felt themselves as though torn away from the traditional relationship with the spiritual world. Human souls who were predestined to become anthroposophists experienced something in the supersensible that had never before been experienced by human souls in those realms during the time between death and a new birth. The earlier experience during the time between death and a new birth had been that human souls worked in concert with the leading spiritual beings to develop the karma for the next Earth existence. But no karma had been worked out in the way the karma was worked out for those who were predestined to become anthroposophists by the things I just mentioned. No work had been done in the Sun region between death and a new birth like the work done now under Michael's regency that had been freed from earthly matters" (CW 240), op cit, p. 187; lecture, July 20, 1924.
107. CW 237, op cit, p. 116; lecture, July 28, 1924.

108. CW 240, op cit, p. 190; lecture, July 20, 1924.
109. CW 237, op cit, pp. 113f; lecture, July 28, 1924; see Rudolf Steiner, "The World-Thoughts in the Working of Michael and in the Working of Ahriman," 16.11.24, in *Anthroposophical Leading Thoughts* (CW 26), pp. 97ff.
110. Ibid., p. 114; lecture, July 28, 1924.
111. CW 240, op cit, p. 213; lecture, Aug. 12, 1924.
112. CW 237, op cit, p. 117; lecture, July 28, 1924.
113. CW 240, op cit, p. 177; lecture, July 19, 1924.
114. CW 238, op cit, p. 92; lecture, Sept. 16, 1924.
115. CW 240, op cit, pp. 179; lecture, July 19, 1924 (emphasis by the author).
116. CW 237, op cit, p. 53; lecture, July 6, 1924 (emphasis by the author).
117. Rudolf Steiner, *Die Verbindung zwischen Lebenden und Toten* [in English: *The Connection between the Living and the Dead*, Great Barrington, MA: SteinerBooks, forthcoming] (CW 168), p. 56; lecture, Feb. 18, 1916.
118. CW 240, p. 145f; lecture, July 8, 1924 (emphasis by the author).
119. CW 237, op cit, p. 53; lecture, July 6, 1924.
120. CW 238, op cit, p. 173; lecture, Sept. 28, 1924.
121. On this "gathering" of people who belong to the destiny group of the Michael stream, see CW 237, op cit, p. 102; lecture, July 1, 1924.
122. Rudolf Steiner to Willem Zeylmans van Emmichoven when they first met in the Dornach Carpentry Building on Dec. 17, 1920. See Peter Selg, *Willem Zeylmans van Emmichoven. Anthroposophie und Anthroposophische Gesellschaft im 20. Jahrhundert* [Willem Zeylmans van Emmichoven. Anthroposophy and the Anthroposophical Society in the 20th century] (Arlesheim, 2009), p. 41. In noting his first impressions as Rudolf Steiner entered to begin his lecture, Zeylmans observed: "It was bitter cold outside; Dornach was covered in snow. Suddenly the blue curtain next to the stage lifted and Rudolf Steiner (whom I knew from pictures) went to the lectern. At that moment I had an immediate experience of recognition. That happened to such an extent that a whole series of images rose up simultaneously, somehow pointing to earlier situations: I see him as my teacher through the millennia. This was the strongest experience I have had in my lifetime. I sat there for a long time as though my mind were elsewhere ..." (ibid., p. 37).
123. On the shared experience of the cultus at the beginning of the nineteenth century and the "streaming together" in the Anthroposophical Society a century later by the human souls that had participated, see CW 240, op cit, p. 145; lecture, July 18, 1924.

124. Rudolf Steiner, *Zur Geschichte und aus den Inhalten der erkenntniskultischen Abteilung der Esoterischen Schule von 1904 bis 1914* [in English: *From the History and Contents of the First Section of the Esoteric School: Letters, Documents, and Lectures: 1904–1914*, Great Barrington, MA: SteinerBooks, 2010] (CW 265), p. 465; also J. Emanuel Zeylmans van Emmichoven, *Strengthening the Heart: A Contemporary Mystery Schooling: Rudolf Steiner's Collaboration with Ita Wegman*, Chestnut Ridge, NY: Mercury Press, 2013, pp. 86ff.
125. See Rudolf Steiner, *Occult History: Historical Personalities and Events in the Light of Spiritual Science*, London: Rudolf Steiner Press, 1957 (CW 126).
126. See Peter Selg, "Rudolf Steiner and the Building of the First Goetheanum" in Sergei O. Prokofieff and Peter Selg, *The Creative Power of Anthroposophical Christology*, Great Barrington, MA: SteinerBooks, 2012, pp. 75ff.
127. See especially the London lecture of May 1 and 2, 1913, and the Stuttgart lecture of May 20, in *Approaching the Mystery of Golgotha*, Great Barrington, MA: SteinerBooks, 2006 (CW 152); see also Andreas Neider, *Michael und die Apokalypse des 20. Jahrhunderts*.
128. Rudolf Steiner, *Die Konstitution der Allgemeinen Anthroposophischen Gesellschaft und der Freien Hochschule für Geisteswissenschaft; Der Wiederaufbau des Goetheanum 1924/25* [in English: *The Foundation Stone / The Life, Nature & Cultivation of Anthroposophy*, London: Rudolf Steiner Press, 2011] (CW 260a), p. 105; lecture, Jan. 18, 1924.
129. CW 237, op cit, p. 140; lecture, Aug. 3, 1924.
130. CW 260a, op cit, p.115; lecture, Jan. 30, 1924.
131. Ibid., p. 270; lecture, Jan. 1, 1924.
132. CW 240, op cit, p. 183; lecture, July 19, 1924.
133. Sergei O. Prokofieff, *Die Esoterik der Anthroposophischen Gesellschaft*, [The esoteric nature of the Anthroposophical Society], p. 23; English edition forthcoming.
134. See Sergei O. Prokofieff, *The First Class of the Michael School and Its Christological Foundations* (Dornach, 2012); and Peter Selg, *Rudolf Steiner and the School for Spiritual Science: The Foundation of the "First Class,"* Great Barrington, MA: SteinerBooks, 2012.
135. See Sergei O. Prokofieff, "The Mystery Act of the Foundation Stone Laying," in *May Human Beings Hear It! The Mystery of the Christmas Conference*, London: Temple Lodge, 2004, pp. 91ff.

136. CW 240, op cit, p. 188; lecture, July 20, 1924.
137. Ibid., p. 157; lecture, July 18, 1924.
138. Rudolf Steiner, *Der Goetheanum-Gedanke inmitten der Kulturkrisis der Gegenwart. Gesammelte Aufsätze aus der Wochenschrift "Das Goetheanum"* 1921–1925 [The idea of the Goetheanum in the midst of the cultural crisis of the present. Collected essays from the weekly "Das Goetheanum" 1921–1925] (CW 36), p. 309.
139. CW 240, op cit, p. 307; lecture, Aug. 27, 1924.
140. CW 237, op cit, p. 142; lecture, Aug. 8,1924.
141. See Peter Selg, *Rudolf Steiner*, vol. 3, pp. 1,959ff.
142. CW 240, op cit, p. 161, lecture of July 18, 1924.
143. Friedrich Rittelmeyer, *Meine Lebensbegegnung mit Rudolf Steiner* [in English: *Rudolf Steiner Enters My Life,* Edinburgh: Floris Books, 2013] (Stuttgart, 1983), pp. 156f.
144. See Sergei O. Prokofieff, "Rudolf Steiner und das Karma der Anthroposophischen Gesellschaft" [Rudolf Steiner and the karma of the Anthroposophical Society] in *Die Esoterik der Anthroposophischen Gesellschaft* [The esoteric nature of the Anthroposophical Society], pp. 107ff (also pp. 117f); English edition forthcoming.
145. Marie Steiner, "An die Mitgliedschaft der Anthroposophischen Gesellschaft in der Schweiz" [To the members of the Anthroposophical Society in Switzerland], in *Das Goetheanum. Nachrichtenblatt für Mitglieder* 51, Dec. 20, 1942.
146. Rudolf Steiner, *From the History and Contents of the First Section of the Esoteric School: Letters, Documents, and Lectures, 1904–1914,* Great Barrington, MA: SteinerBooks, 2010 (CW 266/1); esoteric lesson of Oct. 23, 1907.
147. For a related survey of the twentieth century, see the great study by historian Eric Hobsbawm (1917–2012), *The Age of Extremes: The Short Twentieth Century, 1914–1991* (London, 1994).
148. CW 237, op cit, p. 127; lecture, Aug. 1, 1924; see also Hans Peter van Manen, *Wiederkunft und Heimsuchung* [Return and affliction] (Dornach, 2011); Andreas Neider, *Der Mensch zwischen Über- und Unternatur, Das Erwachen des Bewusstseins im Ätherischen und die Gefährdung der freien Kräfte* [The human being between super-nature and sub-nature. The awakening of consciousness in the etheric and the threat to the forces which are free] (Stuttgart, 2012); Rudolf Steiner, *Der elektronische Doppelgänger und die Entstehung der Computertechnik* [The electronic double and the rise of computer technology], Andreas Neider (ed.) (Basel, 2012).
149. See Peter Selg, *Unbornness: Human Pre-existence and the Journey toward Birth,* Great Barrington, MA: SteinerBooks, 2010, pp. 43ff.

150. CW 237, op cit, p. 136; lecture, Aug. 3, 1924.
151. See Sergei O. Prokofieff, "The Nature of the Christmas Conference and its Sources of Inspiration," in Sergei O. Prokofieff and Peter Selg, *The Creative Power of Anthroposophical Christology*, Great Barrington, MA: SteinerBooks, 2012, pp. 227ff.
152. CW 260a, op cit, p. 99; lecture, Jan. 18, 1924.
153. See Sergei O. Prokofieff, *Die Begegnung mit dem Bösen und seine Überwindung in der Geisteswissenchaft. Der Grundstein des Guten* (Dornach, 2003), p. 87 [in English: *The Encounter with Evil: And Its Overcoming through Spiritual Science*, London: Temple Lodge, 1999, pp. 67ff].
154. Sergei O. Prokofieff, *Wie stehen wir heute vor Rudolf Steiner?* (Arlesheim, 2012), p. 46 [in English: Sergei O. Prokofieff and Peter Selg, *Crisis in the Anthroposophical Society and Pathways to the Future*, part 2, "How Do We Stand Before Rudolf Steiner Today?" London: Temple Lodge, 2013, p. 85].
155. CW 26, op cit, p. 73.
156. Sergei O. Prokofieff, *Die Esoterik der Anthroposophischen Gesellschaft* [The esoteric nature of the Anthroposophical Society], p. 61; English edition forthcoming.
157. Ibid., p. 157.
158. Ibid., p. 125.
159. Ibid., p. 126.
160. CW 240, op cit, p. 183; lecture, July 19, 1924.
161. See Sergei O. Prokofieff, "Das Wesen der Weihnachtstagung und ihre Inspirationsquellen," in Sergei O. Prokofieff and Peter Selg, *Die Weihnachtstagung und die Begründung der neuen Mysterien* (Arlesheim, 2011), pp. 43ff [in English: "The Nature of the Christmas Conference and its Sources of Inspiration," in Sergei O. Prokofieff and Peter Selg, *The Creative Power of Anthroposophical Christology*, Great Barrington, MA: SteinerBooks, 2012, pp. 227ff].
162. CW 240, op cit, p. 307; lecture, Aug. 27, 1924.
163. Sergei O. Prokofieff, *Die Esoterik der Anthroposophischen Gesellschaft*, op cit, p. 163.
164. Madeleine P. van Deventer to Emanuel Zeylmans van Emmichoven, Dec. 27, 1982, Ita Wegman Institute, Arlesheim.
165. Sergei O. Prokofieff, *Die Esoterik der Anthroposophischen Gesellschaft*, op cit, p. 160.
166. Ita Wegman, *An die Freunde. Aufsätze und Berichte aus den Jähren 1925–27* [To the friends. Essays and reports from 1925–1927] (Arlesheim, 1986), p. 38. Selections in English are contained

in (C. Villeneuve, ed.) Ita Wegman, *Esoteric Studies: The Michael Impulse*, Forest Row, UK: Temple Lodge 2013.

167. Sergei O. Prokofieff, *Die Esoterik der Anthroposophischen Gesellschaft*, op cit, p. 80.

168. Rudolf Steiner, *Der Jahreskreislauf als Atmungsvorgang der Erde und die vier großen Festeszeiten* [in English: *The Cycle of the Year as a Breathing Process and the Four Great Festivals,* Hudson, NY: Anthroposophic Press, 1988] (CW 223), p. 118; lecture, Sept. 28, 1913.

169. CW 260, op cit, p. 280; lecture, Jan. 1, 1924.

170. Sergei O. Prokofieff, *Menschen mögen es hören* [in English: *May Human Beings Hear It! The Mystery of the Christmas Conference,* Forest Row, UK: Temple Lodge, 2004, ch. 8, p. 528] (Stuttgart, 2002), p. 619.

171. CW 268, op cit, p. 350.

172. Sergei O. Prokofieff, *Die Esoterik der Anthroposophischen Gesellschaft*, op cit, p. 11.

173. J. Emanuel Zeylmans van Emmichoven, *Strengthening the Heart. A Contemporary Mystery Schooling: Rudolf Steiner's Collaboration with Ita Wegman,* Chestnut Ridge, NY: Mercury Press, 2013, p. 268.

Books in English Translation by Peter Selg

On Rudolf Steiner:

Rudolf Steiner: Life and Work, volume 1 of 7 (2014)
Rudolf Steiner and Christian Rosenkreutz (2012)
Rudolf Steiner as a Spiritual Teacher: From Recollections of Those Who Knew Him (2010)

On Christology:

The Lord's Prayer and Rudolf Steiner: A Study of His Insights into the Archetypal Prayer of Christianity (2014)
The Creative Power of Anthroposophical Christology: An Outline of Occult Science · The First Goetheanum · The Fifth Gospel · The Christmas Conference (with Sergei O. Prokofieff) (2012)
Christ and the Disciples: The Destiny of an Inner Community (2012)
The Figure of Christ: Rudolf Steiner and the Spiritual Intention behind the Goetheanum's Central Work of Art (2009)
Rudolf Steiner and the Fifth Gospel: Insights into a New Understanding of the Christ Mystery
Seeing Christ in Sickness and Healing (2005)

On General Anthroposophy:

The Destiny of the Michael Community: Foundation Stone for the Future (2014)
Spiritual Resistance: Ita Wegman 1933–1935 (2014)
The Last Three Years: Ita Wegman in Ascona, 1940–1943 (2014)
From Gurs to Auschwitz: The Inner Journey of Maria Krehbiel-Darmstädter (2013)
Crisis in the Anthroposophical Society: And Pathways to the Future (2013); with Sergei O. Prokofieff
Rudolf Steiner's Foundation Stone Meditation: And the Destruction of the Twentieth Century (2013)
The Culture of Selflessness: Rudolf Steiner, the Fifth Gospel, and the Time of Extremes (2012)
The Mystery of the Heart: The Sacramental Physiology of the Heart in Aristotle, Thomas Aquinas, and Rudolf Steiner (2012)

Rudolf Steiner and the School for Spiritual Science: The Foundation of the "First Class" (2012)
Rudolf Steiner's Intentions for the Anthroposophical Society: The Executive Council, the School for Spiritual Science, and the Sections (2011)
The Fundamental Social Law: Rudolf Steiner on the Work of the Individual and the Spirit of Community (2011)
The Path of the Soul after Death: The Community of the Living and the Dead as Witnessed by Rudolf Steiner in his Eulogies and Farewell Addresses (2011)
The Agriculture Course, Koberwitz, Whitsun 1924: Rudolf Steiner and the Beginnings of Biodynamics (2010)
Karl König's Path to Anthroposophy (2008)

ON ANTHROPOSOPHICAL MEDICINE AND CURATIVE EDUCATION:

Honoring Life: Medical Ethics and Physician-Assisted Suicide (2014); with Sergei O. Prokofieff
I Am for Going Ahead: Ita Wegman's Work for the Social Ideals of Anthroposophy (2012)
The Child with Special Needs: Letters and Essays on Curative Education (Ed.) (2009)
Ita Wegman and Karl König: Letters and Documents (2008)
Karl König's Path to Anthroposophy (2008)
Karl König: My Task: Autobiography and Biographies (Ed.) (2008)

ON CHILD DEVELOPMENT AND WALDORF EDUCATION:

I Am Different from You: How Children Experience Themselves and the World in the Middle of Childhood (2011)
Unbornness: Human Pre-existence and the Journey toward Birth (2010)
The Essence of Waldorf Education (2010)
The Therapeutic Eye: How Rudolf Steiner Observed Children (2008)
A Grand Metamorphosis: Contributions to the Spiritual-Scientific Anthropology and Education of Adolescents (2008)

Ita Wegman Institute
for Basic Research into Anthroposophy

Pfeffinger Weg 1a, ch 4144 Arlesheim, Switzerland
www.wegmaninstitut.ch
e-mail: sekretariat@wegmaninstitut.ch

The Ita Wegman Institute for Basic Research into Anthroposophy is a non-profit research and teaching organization. It undertakes basic research into the lifework of Dr. Rudolf Steiner (1861–1925) and the application of Anthroposophy in specific areas of life, especially medicine, education, and curative education. Work carried out by the Institute is supported by a number of foundations and organizations and an international group of friends and supporters. The Director of the Institute is Prof. Dr. Peter Selg.

www.ingramcontent.com/pod-product-compliance
Lightning Source LLC
Chambersburg PA
CBHW020947090426
42736CB00010B/1298